HAVE YOU BEEN
TO ROME?

HAVE YOU BEEN TO ROME?

AUGUSTA L. FRANCIS

Foreword By

Rt. Rev. Mgr. Charles L. Duchemin

Protonotary Apostolic
Rector of the Beda College, Rome

LONDON, 1954
SAMUEL WALKER LTD.
(Printers and Publishers)
27 Chancery Lane, W.C.2

NIHIL OBSTAT

        DANIEL DUIVESTEIJN, S.T.D.,

              Censor Deputatus.

IMPRIMATUR

       E. MORROGH BERNARD,

             Vic. Gen.

Westmonasterii, die 27a Aprilis, 1954.

DEDICATION

*To all lovers of the
Eternal City*

Contents

Foreword

HAVE you been to Rome?

If you have, you will enjoy this book as a reminder of what you saw there; and, unless I am mistaken, you will be surprised to learn how much more you *might* have seen had you known where to look.

If you have not been to Rome, and are unable through duties at home, sickness or want of funds to make the journey, then this book will give you the next best thing, a vivid word picture of the real Rome, the centre of Christendom.

If however you are about to go to Rome you will do well to read this book first, then you will be prepared to enjoy Rome to the full.

It consists of some fifty talks (published originally in the *Catholic Fireside*), by someone who has lived in Rome for nearly a quarter of a century, and has entered into and enjoyed every detail of its life. Now a book may be informative yet very dull; a railway time-table, for instance, will tell you accurately the precise time a train should pass this or that point, but will give no idea of the beauty of the scenery. This book which does not claim to be a guide book does however give you accurate information about the marvels of Rome, and at the same time brings Rome to life for you.

The short articles cover the important churches, the chief antiquities, the more outstanding art treasures as well as describing the religious and social practices of Rome, the street shrines and ancient popular devotions. The Vatican, about which it is difficult to get accurate details is fully described with all the reverence it deserves. Not only are there special chapters for the more serious features such as the Basilica of St. Peter's, the Vatican Museums and the Sistine Chapel, but also some short ones giving fascinating and little known facts under such headings as the Vatican Gardens, the Pope's Fire Brigade, the Vatican Daily Newspaper.

Religious Orders that have played such an important part in the development of Rome have separate pages, together with the people and places associated with them.

But it is not the purpose of this introduction to describe the contents of the book, but merely to hint at its merits, while expressing appreciation and gratitude by one who has lived in Rome for over twenty-five years. He looks on it as a genuine service to the Church as well as to scholarship, for it will remain a treasury of delight to many generations and will take away a reproach that he has long felt was only too well founded. It was said that books that gave reliable information about history and archaeology were devoid of all sense of that piety which is an essential for anyone who would really understand Rome. On the other hand pious books were only too frequently entirely inadequate from a scholar's point of view. Here there is a rare combination of easy reading, erudition and true devotion.

CHARLES L. H. DUCHEMIN,

Rector, Pontifical Beda College.

Rome, February 1954.

Rome is 2,706 Years of Age

T HE celebration of the "Birthday of Rome" gives food for thought regarding the age of the Eternal City. She is—according to tradition—exactly 2,706 years of age. And visitors say that she carries them well. She has the secret of perpetual youth, because she is the heart of the world, the residence of the Vicar of Christ on Earth, hallowed by the blood of martyrs and the lives of countless saints.

Our photograph is symbolic, for it shows the arch of Constantine, beneath which some Passionist Fathers are approaching. It commemorated the victory of the Emperor Constantine over his enemies in 312; and in consequence of this victory, Christianity was thenceforward not only tolerated but honoured and encouraged.

This toleration was due to the fact that during the Battle of the Milvian Bridge the Emperor had a vision of the Cross in the heavens, and near it the words: "By this Sign thou shalt conquer". It has been well said that the arch is a portal between two worlds: that of paganism and that of Christianity.

It is the last of all Roman triumphal arches, decorated with reliefs taken from the great Temple of Apollo on the Palatine Hill; but in reality it represents victorious Christianity.

To return, however, to the origin of the city and to the well-known legend of the twin brothers; Romulus and Remus. It is related in ancient chronicles that the Vestal, Rhea Silva, after her union with the god Mars, gave birth to twin sons, Romulus and Remus. The children were ordered to be drowned in the Tiber, but were miraculously saved and tended by a she-wolf in a cave of the Palatine Hill.

When grown to manhood they determined to found a

city on the banks of the Tiber; but they quarrelled in the process and Remus was slain. Romulus, nevertheless, founded the city in the year 752 before the birth of Our Lord.

The rising City-State was governed by kings, then as a republic by magistrates, then by emperors. And under

The Arch of Constantine—portal between paganism and Christianity

the latter its dominion extended over most of the known world which centred around the Mediterranean. At that time were built the roads, the famous highways of stone or flint (as seen in the foreground of our illustration), reaching to the uttermost boundaries of the Empire and along which travelled eventually, not only conquering legions, but the messengers of the Gospel.

The blood of the martyrs shed during the Imperial persecutions was truly the seed of the Church, and the waves of conversions which followed the persecutions culminated, one may say, in the conversion of the Emperor Constantine.

In this way, Christianity came up above ground from the catacombs, freed from the nightmare of persecution. Carried away by enthusiasm not only did the Emperor permit the erection of noble basilicas, but we are told that he worked at the construction of the Lateran Basilica with his own hands.

He had begun by summoning Pope St. Sylvester back to Rome from a cave on Mount Soracte, where the latter had been persuaded to hide from persecution. An old legend relates that the Pope could not believe the messengers who brought the Emperor's summons to return confidently to Rome to receive the rich gifts and property connected with the Lateran buildings. So St. Sylvester tarried on his mountain.

More messengers were sent by the impatient Constantine, who at last convinced the Pontiff, and presented him with a fine, strong mule for the journey—a distance of about twenty-five miles. But the Pope did not wish to keep the Emperor waiting any longer; so, obedient to his saintly rider, that mule took off from the summit of the mountain and in three mighty leaps reached Rome.

And to the incredulous in need of being convinced, the inhabitants of the intervening villages point out the spots where the mule left the hoof-marks of his two landings between the points of departure and arrival.

Less doubtful, however, than the achievement of Pope St. Sylvester's mule is the laying of the foundations of the great Roman Constantinian basilicas.

They are astounding to the pilgrim who comes to realise the riches and the beauty of the churches which arose in majesty during the second half of the fourth century. The Lateran Basilica (the Pope's Cathedral Church to this day) was begun, as were St. Peter's, St. Mary Major, St. Paul's-Outside-the-Walls, St. Lawrence-Outside-the-Walls,

Holy Cross-in-Jerusalem, St. Clement's, St. Martin-on-the-Hill, St. Pudentiana and St. Praxedes, merely to mention the most important.

Of course, many of these buildings have been reconstructed and restored; they have been decorated anew and many things in them have been altered. But as a rule at least the Constantinian foundations can be seen; the general outline is the same, and the burial-place of the martyr below the high altar is unchanged.

St. Mary Major—Our Lady's Greatest Church

ST. MARY MAJOR may well be called "St. Mary's the Great" for it is the greatest church in the whole world dedicated to Our Lady, and as such takes precedence of all the others, excepting Loreto, which ranks first. It is interesting to note in this connection that there are a great many other churches in Rome dedicated to the Mother of God.

When you have visited St. Peter's, St. John Lateran, St. Paul's-Outside-the-Walls and St. Mary Major, then you will have seen the most significant places of all in the Eternal City.

In a series of considerations on these basilicas it is useful to keep in mind just why they are classed as "major". They are among the most ancient in Rome, of course, but beyond the dignity due to antiquity, each has its special claim to be called "greater" or "major".

St. Peter's is built over the tomb of the Prince of the Apostles; St. Paul's over the tomb of St. Paul; St. John Lateran is the Pope's Cathedral as Bishop of Rome, and enshrines the heads of both St. Peter and St. Paul; St. Mary Major is the first great church built in honour of Our Lady and guards the relics of the Crib of Bethlehem.

Of the four, the last named is the only one that has not been rebuilt. It will be remembered that by 1500 the foundations of St. Peter's had given way and that it took 100 years to reconstruct it and add the great dome; in 1348 both earthquake and fire damaged the Lateran Basilica so seriously that it had to be rebuilt entirely on the ancient foundations; and in 1823 St. Paul's was destroyed by fire, and was afterwards reconstructed.

Therefore, on entering *Santa Maria Maggiore*, the pilgrim

might perhaps pause for a minute to let the impression of the majestic dignity of the great pillared space sink into his soul, together with the thought that, like a sea of prayer, continuous tides of petition, adoration, love and contrition have been, as it were, washing around the bases of those stately columns.   I do not think that one need necessarily be "psychic" or particularly "sensitive to places" (what-

The Basilica of St. Mary Major

ever those expressions may mean) to feel and know that in this basilica the prayers of the faithful have risen to Heaven for sixteen centuries.

The original building was erected, according to the oft-repeated legend, in consequence of a dream sent on the night of August 4th in the year 358, to a certain Roman noble named John, and also to Pope Liberius. In this dream Our Lady let each know that she wished a church to be built in her honour on the Esquiline Hill, on a spot which should be marked by a fall of snow.

Pilgrims who are brave enough to defy tropical heat and to come in August, will easily be convinced of the miraculous nature of snow in Rome during that particular month.

On August 5th, then, they went to the Esquiline, found a small snow-field on the summit, and in it, with the foot of his pastoral staff, the Pope drew the outline of the church. That, then, is the origin of the Feast of Our Lady of the Snow.

Each year during High Mass there, on that day, a shower of white rose petals falls gently from the roof on to the congregation in remembrance of the event.

About eighty years later, after the Council of Ephesus (432) triumphantly declared Our Lady to be Mother of Jesus Christ as God as well as Man, Pope Sixtus III rebuilt and enlarged it, in the form we see today. And in the centre of the magnificent mosaic arch which surmounts the Pontifical Altar he caused his name to be inscribed: *"Sixtus III Servant of the Servants of God"*.

Directly below the Pontifical Altar are kept the relics of the Crib of Bethlehem in a valuable crystal and gold reliquary. Someone has called them "the most sacred bundle of sticks in existence". There are a few pieces of wood, only; the crib itself is not complete, but these relics of it are among the holiest relics in the world.

It is impossible to do more than touch on the salient features of this glorious basilica. Because it was "protected" by Spain, the first Spanish gentlemen-adventurers, the forerunners of Raleigh, Drake and Hawkins, who went out to the New World and brought back shiploads of precious metals and stones, offered the first gold nuggets to gild the ceiling of St. Mary Major.

The gold is still there, as bright and as handsome as on the first day it was put to such a noble purpose.

Of the two chapels, which seem to be transepts, but which were in reality added in the sixteenth century, one is used for the Blessed Sacrament and the other for the most ancient picture of Our Lady which is in Rome. They contain untold treasures in the way of relics and works of art.

We may not linger to describe in detail how the body of the Apostle St. Matthias lies beneath the altar of the Crib; nor how the body of St. Jerome is buried "somewhere" beneath the pavement, no one quite knows where; nor how the great St. Cajetan, praying before the Crib on Christmas night in 1517, received the Divine Infant in his arms; nor how St. Ignatius Loyola there celebrated his first Mass.

Particularly interesting to English pilgrims, among the treasures here preserved, is the dalmatic worn by St. Thomas of Canterbury when he was struck down in his cathedral, and upon which bloodstains are still visible. This precious vestment was brought to the Pope soon after the martyrdom, and the Pope gave it into the custody of the Canons of St. Mary Major. It is difficult to obtain the privilege of venerating this relic, but possibly at some later period, pilgrims may be allowed to do so.

Our Lady has 137 Churches in Rome

DEVOTION to Our Lady is more conspicuous in Rome than in any other city in the world. That is, of course, as it should be.

Besides the two huge Corinthian columns bearing her statue—one in Piazza di Spagna, the other in front of St. Mary Major—and besides the eight hundred wayside shrines or "little Madonnas" (*Madonelle*), as they are called, she has no less than one hundred and thirty-seven churches dedicated to her; that is to say, a little more than a third of Rome's four hundred and fifty churches. It would be wearisome to enumerate them all, but a few are of special interest.

The following, be it noted, are real churches. Besides these are two hundred and eighty-seven chapels open to the public. And the chapels which are classed as "private", belonging to religious institutions and not open to the public, have, one might imagine, never been really counted.

Numerically, "Our Lady of the Rosary" leads, with six churches. "Our Lady of Providence" follows with five. Four each are dedicated to "Our Lady of Salvation" and to "Our Lady of Mount Carmel". There are three of "Our Lady of Loreto", and also three of "Our Lady of Mercy".

Then follow the wonderful "single" churches, beginning of course, with St. Mary Major, queen of them all.. On the evening of the declaration of the dogma of the Assumption the illuminations at St. Mary Major surpassed everything else in the city, except perhaps St. Peter's and Castle Sant' Angelo. The lines of façade and portico were outlined in living flame, the great mosaics of the loggia blazed in all their magnificence of gold and colour, under powerful floodlights.   The bell-tower seemed to be some fairy construction rising above the basilica, turned to a pillar of flame by floodlights from the square below.   The interior blazed, too, with light and colour.   Certainly in

The 1400 year old church of Santa Maria in Cosmedin—
"Our Lady the Beautiful"

every sense St. Mary Major queened it over the whole of Rome on that historic evening.

"Our Lady of the Angels" is dedicated to her because of the vision in which she appeared to St. Bernard surrounded by angels; it was formerly a very pagan place too, for the building was erected by the Emperor Diocletian and used as *thermae* or baths; in its construction he employed several thousand Christians, who were afterwards cruelly put to death. St. Bernard's monks came to occupy the premises as a monastery and a church in the sixteenth century, thus recalling their Founder's vision. It is the first church which meets the eye of the traveller emerging from the railway station; and offers a fitting welcome to the Eternal City.

There is "St. Mary the Ancient" in the Roman Forum (no longer used as a church), but at the opposite end of the Forum is "St. Mary the New", built in A.D. 850 because the former had been damaged by earthquakes. The latter is under the care of the Olivetan monks, and St. Frances of Rome is buried beneath the high altar.

"*Santa Maria di Ara Coeli*" ("St. Mary's of the Altar of Heaven") is the church dedicated by St. Helena on the spot where Augustus raised an altar to an Unknown God who was to be born of a Virgin. It is also the church of the "Commune of Rome", or the County Council. The mayor and city officials are present at Mass there on great public occasions, for it stands on the Capitol near the Council's meeting-place. At *Santa Maria in Campitelli* ("St. Mary's of the Little Field")—because the church *was* built in a little field—every Saturday, special prayers are said for the conversion of England before the miraculous picture of Our Lady. This devotion was established by King James III.

Then there is the lovely church near the Tiber, its name derived from the Greek: "St. Mary the Beautiful" (*Santa Maria in Cosmedin*), which stands guard over two pagan temples, with its soaring bell-tower and its exquisite ornamental sculpture. "St. Mary's of the Lady Cyriaca" (*Santa Maria in Dominica*) crowns the Caelian Hill, and records the fact that the property was owned by a great lady called Cyriaca, who gave her goods to the poor through no less a person than St. Lawrence.

"St. Mary's - Over - Minerva" (*"Santa Maria Sopra Minerva"*) has a ring of triumph in its name; it was built in 1285, literally on top of the ruins of a great temple of Minerva, raised by Pompey in memory of his military successes in Asia. It has always been under the care of the Dominican Fathers. The body of St. Catherine of Siena lies beneath the high altar. It was her favourite church, and she died in a neighbouring convent.

The graceful little church of "St. Mary of Peace" stands in an ancient square in one of the oldest and most unchanged parts of medieval Rome. Its portico is the object of unlimited admiration on the part of visiting architects, for it is set in the little *piazza* like a jewel in a ring. Newly-married couples go there to pray before Our Lady's picture for peace in their future lives; and it is said that she grants their petitions. From the artistic point of view, as well as the architectural it is most important. Raphael himself was called in to decorate the walls, and he painted four majestic Sibyls receiving revelations from angels regarding the birth of Our Lord. Bramante designed the adjoining cloister, and Peruzzi and Maratta continued the work of decoration begun by Raphael.

A pilgrimage to all the churches dedicated to the Mother of God in the Eternal City, would be a means of showing devotion to her and of increasing one's knowledge of her. Pilgrimages will never come to an end, on the contrary, they are increasing. And since all roads lead to Rome, why not come to honour Our Lady very specially in that way? Yet, if this should be impossible, the pilgrimage may be made in spirit, as it may be made to any one of her other shrines; for indeed she is "Our Lady of Everywhere".

Street Shrines of Our Lady

WHEN you come to Rome it is safe to say that many things will surprise you.

Many details you will already be prepared for; and the great "occasions" such as Mass in St. Peter's said by the Holy Father, your first visit to the Catacombs, or the sight of the Colosseum, you will already have anticipated in imagination.

It is our intention, however, to describe some of these many delightful features of which, perhaps, you have never dreamed. Among these features are the thousand or so, little shrines of Our Lady to be seen everywhere, if only you remember to look *up*!

When you walk about the streets of Rome (especially the narrower ones) you may answer that you are so busy dodging the traffic in a place where there is only roadway and no sidewalk for pedestrians, that you have no time to raise your eyes. That may be. In which case you might seek the shelter of the entrance to some great *palazzo* or palace, to be found in nearly every Roman street; and there, safe from bicycles and motor cars (not to mention the antiquated one-horse *carozze* and wine carts), you might raise your eyes to the surrounding walls where you are certain to find a picture of Our Lady painted on one of them, or in a niche.

Some of the pictures are surrounded by *ex-votos,* small marble tablets expressing gratitude. Some are roughly executed in paint or sculpture. Some are small masterpieces of Renaissance art. Most of them have little lights burning in front. Many more have flowers, in either china vases or (I regret to say) tin cans. Whatever the container of the blossoms may be, it nevertheless speaks of a simple devotion to the Mother of God.

Some have carved inscriptions beneath them, stating what indulgences have been granted for the recitation of certain prayers (nearly always three Hail Marys) before the shrine. Sometimes even, there are low marble

benches at the foot of the wall, where it is not unusual to
see figures kneeling in prayer. The number of men who
take off their hats when passing these shrines is remarkable.

Some of the pictures are recognised by the ecclesiastical
authority as ''miraculous'' and have been crowned by
the diocesan clergy. In some cases, the miraculous pictures
have been removed from the outer walls where they were
originally located, and placed inside churches for greater
safety.

This is the case with the famous *Madonna della Strada*
which stood at a street corner near the site of the famous
Jesuit church of the Holy Name, and which was removed
from its original position and placed in a richly decorated
chapel in the church itself, where it is to be seen to this
day.

Our Lady of the Street (a more correct translation of

Two angels support this picture of Our Lady

Madonna della Strada than "Our Lady of the Wayside")
is the special patroness of the Roman street-cleaners who
meet periodically at her shrine for devotions and for week-
end retreats.

In the middle ages, before cities were regularly lit, and
when link-boys used to accompany their patrons when
they went abroad after dark, the only street lighting consisted of the lamps which burned before these shrines of
Our Lady.   Today, as already mentioned, although the
streets are brightly lit, yet the tiny flame of a lamp
continues to burn before a number of the Roman
Madonnas.

Our photograph shows a typical shrine of Our Lady in
a busy thoroughfare.   It is placed at the corner of a
building in the *Piazza della Fontana di Trevi;* close to the
renowned fountain into which you must throw a few coins
before you leave Rome, because whoever does this is sure
to return.   The picture is framed in stars and golden rays
and is supported by two angels of the Bernini school.   At
the base of the altar may be seen a few flowers placed there
to honour Our Lady.   And (very practical and modern
detail) in the background several traffic signs appear for
the regulation of motor traffic in particular.   It is this
mingling of old and new, of mysticism and hard-headed
efficiency, that makes these indications of childlike prayer-
fulness all the more thrilling in Italy.

There are twenty-two "regions" or "wards" in Rome,
and each one has its specially cherished Madonnas.   Thus
the one painted on the corner of a building on the Island
in the Tiber, just after you cross the bridge from the right
bank of the river, claims to be the oldest of all; she has
been restored lately and smiles down on passers-by just
as she did many centuries ago.

It is safe to say that miraculous occurrences are
associated with nearly every one of these pictures, for Our
Lady's power is ever manifest, especially where her
children show childlike faith and trust in her.

Rome Consecrated to Our Lady

ONE of the recent public acts of devotion to Our Lady in Rome, was the solemn consecration of the city to her Immaculate Heart. The consecration was made, not by a Cardinal or high ecclesiastical dignitary but, as was the custom in the middle ages when the "free commune of Rome" was all-powerful, it was made by the Mayor, in presence of Church dignitaries and of the population of the city.

During the ceremony it seemed as if the entire two million inhabitants of Rome had gathered in front of the *Ara Coeli* and in the neighbouring streets. When Rome turns out as a whole it really does turn out, that is all one can say.

The occasion was the six hundredth anniversary of the deliverance of Rome from the plague, through the intercession of the Mother of God in the fourteenth century, when the "Black Death" swept through Europe, not sparing England, and leaving a trail of misery and destitution. There were some cases in Rome, but Our Lady came to the rescue.

After Solemn Pontifical Vespers on the day of the consecration, a great procession made its way along the wide (and sometimes narrow) streets which surround the Capitoline Hill. It seemed as if the people could not do enough to honour Our Lady. Flowers and bay leaves were strewn along the roadway, and flowers were scattered from the windows as the ancient picture of the Queen of Heaven passed. Draperies and hangings of all kinds ornamented the houses, and the Standard of Rome was carried proudly by liveried "servants of the Commune".

When the procession finally returned to the church a sermon was preached on Our Lady's protection, and on brotherly love, on the Great Commandment "Thou shalt love thy neighbour as thyself'', and the inexhaustible theme of "peace to men of goodwill", while thousands listened spellbound.

Then came the culminating moment of the day. The Mayor of Rome, flanked by the civic authorities, and speaking in the name of the Roman people, read a solemn act of consecration of the city to the Immaculate Heart of

A flight of marble steps (on the left) lead up to the "Ara Coeli"

Mary. When he had ended, a roar of acclamation resounded and echoed back from the ancient walls of church and Capitol.

The picture of Our Lady which was carried in the procession was painted about nine hundred years ago, and was placed over the high altar of the *Ara Coeli* in the eleventh century, while the church was under the care of Benedictine monks. After the death of St. Francis of Assisi, in the thirteenth century, the Pope gave it to the Franciscans who have remained in possession ever since.

The *Ara Coeli* stands on the Capitoline Hill which was the heart of ancient Rome; the Roman Senate met there, and because all civic life centred there, any religious ceremony that concerns the "people of Rome" as such today, always takes place in the *Ara Coeli*. In other words it is the headquarters of those who write proudly on public buildings as well as on trams and buses the ancient Roman initials "S.P.Q.R.", standing for the Latin words "The Senate and the Roman People".

Our Lady's Christmas Church

VIA DELLA LUNGARETTA "the longish street" if one can translate freely was so named because it was *not* the "really long street". *Via della Lungara*. It runs directly to *Piazza Santa Maria in Trastevere,* where stands a beautiful church dedicated to Our Lady.

The region " Across-the-Tiber", *Trastevere,* has preserved its medieval features better than almost any other part of the Eternal City. It is very ancient, and under the Roman Republic was famous for its gardens. In fact it was there that Julius Caesar owned the gardens which he gave to the Roman people: " . . . *All his walks, His private arbours and new-planted orchards On this side Tiber; he hath left them you, And to your heirs forever— common pleasures, To walk abroad and recreate your- selves . . .* " (Julius Caesar, Act III, Scene 2).

There is a tradition that exactly on Christmas Day, when Our Lord was born in Bethlehem, a spring of oil appeared miraculously on this spot and flowed down to the Tiber for several days. The Christians always held that it was, so to speak, a Christmas present sent by Divine Providence to pagan Rome.

In the reign of Pope St. Callistus I (217—222) the Christians had raised a small oratory on the spot in honour of Our Blessed Lady; therefore this was a place of prayer dedicated to her over a century before St. Mary Major was built.

The ancient chronicles relate that local wine-merchants and tavern-keepers disputed with the Christians for the possession of the place which apparently was considered most desirable, and that they carried their quarrel to the Emperor Alexander Severus. The Emperor answered roundly that he preferred that it should belong to those who honoured God, whatever their form of worship might

c

be, rather than to people who encouraged rioting and drunkenness.

This Emperor, like his predecessor, was always favourable to Eastern religions; he had some vague notion of an Almighty Power, and was sympathetic to all who worshipped such a Power. It was on account of this spirit

Santa Maria in Trastevere—"Our Lady Across the Tiber"

of toleration that Pope St. Callistus was able to organise the Christian possessions, and make some beginning of "Titles", with that of this Christian oratory.

He was also able to superintend the development of the Christian burial-place on the Appian Way, which is to this day known as the Catacomb of St. Callistus. In a part of it, called "the crypt of the Popes" all the pontiffs from Zephyrinus to Eutychian were buried, except Cornelius and Callistus himself. He is said to have extended and unified the cemetery, bringing the isolated private plots into communal possession, making it the first property in land, to be held by the Church.

The close connection of *Santa Maria in Trastevere* with the Nativity is further emphasised by the fact that it is the Stational Church for New Year's Day, Octave of the Nativity and Feast of the Circumcision, linked in a special manner with the Holy Name of Jesus.

Our illustration shows the front of the church dominated by a graceful bell-tower, with the square in front of it ornamented by a characteristically Roman fountain. Considering the façade, the interior, the bell-tower and the position, it is true to say that after St. Mary Major this is the finest church in the city, among those dedicated to Our Lady.

The band of frescoes beneath the triangular pediment show the Infant Christ in His Mother's arms, while on either side the Wise Virgins, carrying lamps, approach to worship Him. It is possible that the Wise Virgins who, it will be remembered, had oil in their lamps ready for the Bridegroom's coming, may be represented here in relation to the miraculous fount of oil which sprang up on the first Christmas Day.

Inside the portico are beautiful paintings of the Annunciation and the Nativity. On entering the church itself we are struck by the magnificence of the polychrome pavement, the ancient marble columns, the superb mosaics, and the ceiling painted by the great Domenichino, of the school of Raphael. In the centre of the ceiling we see Our Lady in glory assumed into Heaven.

The apse, or semicircular ending of the church, with its wonderful mosaics by Cavallini, dating from the thirteenth century, is its crowning glory. Our Lady and her divine Son are seen in the centre, framed by the prophets who announced the Birth of the Saviour.

In smaller panels surrounding and completing the central scene, the life of the Blessed Virgin is briefly represented. There is her birth, followed by the Annunciation, then the Nativity, where, in the background, can be seen a tiny oratory with a small stream flowing from it. Here is clearly an allusion to the fountain of oil. The small panels surround a circular mosaic of Our Lady with the Apostles on either hand.

Two side chapels each enclose a miraculous picture of Our Lady. One known as the *Madonna della Strada Cupa* (the "Madonna of the Dark Street") was brought thither from a street corner where it was formerly honoured. The other enshrines "Our Lady of Mercy", dating from the eighth century.

In front of the main altar, a little to the right, is the famous marble slab, inscribed *"Fons Olei"* which marks the spot whence the "Christmas oil" flowed.

Our Lady of the Three Fountains

OUR LADY has appeared within the last few years in a number of places in Italy; or rather we should put it: "is said to have appeared", for the Church has not made any official pronouncements as yet regarding these apparitions. On the other hand, the Church authorities have not forbidden the faithful meeting in these places to honour Our Lady, and to invoke her intercession. That in itself means a great deal; for when ecclesiastical authority says "yes" the process is always a slow one; whereas when the answer is "no" it usually comes swiftly.

Rome has been specially honoured by Our Lady having appeared in a cave surrounded by a grove of eucalyptus trees, close to the ancient Cistercian Abbey of "Three Fountains". This Abbey is on the site of St. Paul's martyrdom, where three miraculous fountains sprang up on the three points where his head fell and rebounded after it was severed from his body.

The Blessed Virgin appeared for the first time on April 12th, 1947, to an apostate bus-conductor, one Bruno Cornacchiola, and to his three children, respectively four, six, and ten years of age.

Bruno had been persuaded to join the Seventh Day Adventists, and to devote himself as much as possible to fierce anti-Catholic propaganda. It happened that he had a holiday on that memorable April 12th, and took his children to play in the woods at *Tre Fontane*.

As he sat in the shade of a tree, preparing a violent speech against the devotion of Catholics to the Blessed Virgin, he noticed that his children had disappeared into a nearby cave; then he heard them shouting that they had lost their ball, asking him to come and help them.

On approaching the cave he saw one of the three children on his knees murmuring "beautiful lady", with his hands joined as if in prayer, and his eyes fixed on a point in

front and above.   He called the other two, who, as soon
as they entered the cave did the same as the first. Suddenly,
Bruno himself says that he felt as if two gentle hands
were pressed against his closed eyes; when they were

The statue of Our Lady of the Three Fountains in
the Grotto where she appeared.

removed it seemed as if a veil had been torn aside.
    He also saw a "beautiful lady" clad in a white tunic
and a long green cloak.   She wore a deep rose-coloured
girdle, her feet were bare and in her hand was a book with
a grey cover.   She was surrounded with light.

Bruno knelt there for an hour, during which time she spoke to him; but she allowed him to reveal to all only the following words : "I am she who is in the Blessed Trinity. I am the Blessed Virgin of the Revelation. Until today you have persecuted me. Now you must stop, and enter the true fold . . . Words spoken by God Himself will always be fulfilled. Once you made the nine Fridays in honour of the Sacred Heart and that has saved you."

The rest of the "revelation" that she made to Bruno during that hour is, he said, only to be divulged to ecclesiastical authority. Our Lady bade him go for help to a priest who, when greeted, should answer "Ave Maria, my son", and she added that that particular priest would introduce him to another priest who would receive him back into the Church.

A changed man, Bruno returned to his work on the bus. For several weeks he spoke politely to each priest he met, but none of them returned his greeting as Our Lady had said. However, finally, in his parish church, not far from *Tre Fontane,* a young priest answered him in exactly the words Our Lady had indicated, and introduced him to another older priest of the parish, who instructed and absolved him.

Owing to exigencies of space the story has been shortened, but told in full it is dramatic, especially on the occasions when father and children returned to the grotto.

A statue of Our Lady, carved in wood and coloured according to the descriptions given by the children and Bruno, now stands in the cave; it is surrounded with lights and flowers, and numbers of devout clients of Our Lady reverently visit it.

During her apparition Our Lady gave Bruno to understand that prayer and penance were essential to the conversion of the world today, and that she would cure bodily ills through the earth of the grotto. It is significant that, as at Lourdes Our Lady works miracles by means of water, here she does it by means of earth. It is beautiful golden-brown *pozzolana* or dry volcanic soil. The rock of the cave is also volcanic, being the Roman *tufo*.

Certainly, since the first apparition, many miraculous cures have been wrought through the invocation of "Our Lady of the Revelation" (or "Our Lady of the Three Fountains"), not to mention conversions, such as that of George Luzi, a violent "anti-clerical" miraculously cured of varicose veins.

There is a well-attested list of these cures available; they range from Pott's disease and tuberculosis, to paralysis and tumour of the brain. Small quantities of earth from the grotto have been sent far and wide, and accounts of miracles in distant places are already becoming known. One of the most recent was worked in England.

The grotto has been faced with small stone blocks, and an iron grille protects it from the exuberance of over-enthusiastic pilgrims. *Ex-votos*, lights and flowers surround the statue, which is appealing in its simplicity; and Our Lady's clients stretch out their hands and help themselves to earth from the floor of the cave.

St. John Lateran—The Pope's Cathedral Church

WHY are there four major Basilicas and not seven or nine or twelve or two? And what *is* a basilica, when all is said and done? Is there anything symbolic about the number four?

These most reasonable questions are often asked by pilgrims.

Certainly there is some symbolism in the "perfect" number according to the Greek philosopher; there are the four quarters of the globe, the four winds of heaven; and for us Christians the four horsemen of the Apocalypse, the four Evangelists and the four extremities of the Cross of Our Saviour. But even considering these and other examples of the use of the mystic number four, there seems to be no evidence that the four basilicas were planned deliberately.

A "basilica" properly so called (apart from architectural considerations) is a church which has received the title of such from the Pope, granted as a privilege on account of antiquity or historical associations. Basilicas are privileged with the right of precedence as churches, special insignia, and a college of clergy who wear the rochet and *cappa*. There are several "minor" basilicas in Rome and a certain number in other places, but there are only four major basilicas.

They are: St. John Lateran, St. Peter's, St. Paul's-Outside-the-Walls and St. Mary Major. Each of these is of major importance on account of antiquity and the dignity of its associations.

Such was the importance attached to them in the middle ages that the four great Christian Powers each protected one of them. England protected St. Paul's; France,

St. John Lateran; Austria, St. Peter's; and Spain, St. Mary Major.

First in dignity comes St. John Lateran, because it is the Cathedral church of the Bishop of Rome, that is to say it is the Pope's own Cathedral. It is, therefore truly, as stated in the majestic inscriptions on the façade: "The Mistress and Mother of All the Churches".

St. John Lateran, first in dignity of the four Major Basilicas, is the Pope's own Cathedral

Why not St. Peter's? is often asked.   And why is it dedicated to St. John?   And what sort of Saint was "Lateran"?

In reply to the first: it was built before St. Peter's; it was the first great Christian church to be raised by the converted Emperor Constantine, when at last Christianity came into the open light of day. It is said that the Emperor worked on its construction with his own hands, like any ordinary labourer; and when it was finished he presented it solemnly to Pope St. Sylvester, together with much property and many privileges.

Constantine followed the construction of the Lateran by a number of other churches, but the Lateran Basilica was the first. It was originally dedicated to Our Lord under the title of "St. Saviour's", but, as the centuries passed and as Christians realised that all churches in all places were built in honour of God made Man, it was decided to give it the title of both St. Johns who were closely connected with Our Lord when He was on earth.

In consequence, it is dedicated to St. John the Baptist and to St. John the Evangelist as well. The distinguishing name of "Lateran" was used simply because the property on which it was built had belonged to the powerful and rich Roman family of the Laterani, who conspired against Nero, and whose possessions had been forfeited to the Imperial Crown. Hence, Constantine gave the Pope a piece of Imperial property for the site of the basilica.

Because of its dignity, the basilica possesses the inestimably venerable relics of the heads of both St. Peter and St. Paul. There is no question as to their authenticity. They are kept in reliquaries of gold and silver, shaped as portrait-heads of the two Apostles, and placed in the upper section of the canopy which surmounts the Papal altar. As a rule they are curtained off, but on great feasts the curtains are drawn back.

As seen today, the Lateran (as it is frequently called by abbreviation) is not the same as the original church, consecrated by Pope St. Sylvester in the year 324. Since that date it has been burnt, re-built, sacked by barbarians, damaged by earthquake, and repeatedly restored and enlarged. The interior, though smaller than St. Peter's, is impressive.

Beneath the papal altar (behind small bronze doors) is

the original wooden altar used by St. Peter himself and by some of his successors in the catacombs.

High above the tabernacle of the altar in the transept, in a curtained recess, is a plain wooden slab which, tradition also tells us, was the table of the Last Supper at which Our Divine Lord instituted the Holy Eucharist. Nearby, on the left, is the entrance to the cloister which an attendant will open on request. It should not be missed as it is one of the most beautiful in Rome, having been built by the Benedictines of Monte Cassino, in the thirteenth century.

The Holy Stairs

DURING a pilgrimage no one will miss ascending the *Scala Sancta* on bended knees. The indulgences attached to this devotion are many and great. As far back as the year 1100, Pope Paschal II by a bull, dated August 5th, granted an indulgence of nine years for each of the twenty-eight steps, to be gained by those who ascended them on their knees, "praying or meditating on the Passion, with a contrite heart". On September 2nd, 1817, Pope Pius VII confirmed this indulgence.

The Popes have always been attached to the *Scala Sancta* and it is significant to note that today the Passionist Fathers have charge of it, as well as of the neighbouring church of SS. John and Paul. When Pope Pius XII was Cardinal Pacelli he was titular of the latter church. Pope Pius IX himself placed the Holy Stairs under the care of the Passionists. It is said that during the jubilee of the year 1600, Pope Clement VIII ascended them more than sixty times; that is to say, a little more than once a week.

What exactly is this famous staircase? It is nothing less than the flight of twenty-eight marble steps which, tradition tells us, were those of Pilate's palace in Jerusalem, which were ascended and descended by Our Blessed Lord during His trials. There is evidence in favour of their having been brought from the Holy Land by St. Helena, mother of the Emperor Constantine, in the year A.D. 326. Therefore, they have been venerated, most probably, for over 1600 years. Before the rebuilding of the Lateran Basilica in the sixteenth century they stood on the right of the portico.

When alterations were made in the basilica the Holy Stairs were moved to their present position in a specially constructed building on the opposite side of the square. This building shelters not only the *Scala Sancta* but one of the most significant portions of the old Lateran Palace: the *Sancta Sanctorum.*

Pilgrims ascending the Holy Stairs on their knees

This beautiful little chapel may be seen only through the iron grating at the head of the stairs.   Until 1308 it was the private oratory of the Popes, and it was the only part of the Lateran Palace that escaped the great fire of that year.   It contains the famous Greek picture of Our

Lord known as the _Acheiropita_ ("not painted by mortal hand").

The first occasion on which this picture was solemnly carried in procession, was during the Lombard invasion in 754, and the last was in honour of the fifteen hundredth anniversary of the Council of Ephesus, in 1931.

Among the relics of the Passion contained in the chapel are a large piece of the wood of the Cross; a portion of the lance of Longinus which pierced the side of Our Lord; one of the reeds used to strike Him during the night of Maundy Thursday; part of the sponge used to offer Him vinegar during the Crucifixion, and one of the thorns from the Crown of Thorns.

These relics placed in the _Sancta Sanctorum,_ at the head of the Holy Stairs, give added devotion and importance to the act of ascending them. The ascent is, as it were, to Calvary, since so many holy things from Calvary are kept in the shrine. No one ever treads on the Holy Stairs as mentioned above; the faithful go up on their knees. To facilitate the descent there are two flights of stairs built on either side of the _Scala Sancta_ itself.

At times of special devotion, however, the indulgence is extended to these two staircases, and they also are ascended kneeling. For such occasions two additional flights of steps have been provided, beyond the central ones, so that the devout pilgrims may walk down after gaining the indulgence.

The Holy Stairs themselves are covered with wood for protection; in several places small panes of glass have been let into the woodwork, over the marks said to have been left by the bleeding Feet of the Son of God as He descended them.

One of the sights of Rome never enjoyed by the casual tourist, is that of the _Scala Sancta_ on Good Friday. From four o'clock in the morning crowds come to ascend the stairs, devoutly kissing the marks of Our Lord's footsteps. So great are the numbers, that it may be said that the ascent is made by masses of people moving rhythmically, shoulder to shoulder, in an atmosphere of prayer and penance.

We are fortunate in having secured a photograph of a group of peasants making the ascent. Certainly nothing could be more prayerful than their attitudes and expressions. In the illustration of the faithful on the steps, one of the spots marked by the stains of the Blood of Jesus Christ, is seen in the immediate foreground. The glass which protects it is surrounded by a circle of metal set in a cross.

One should allow half an hour for the ascent, as special prayers are said on each step. The experience is unforgettable, and even if one did not know the history of the Stairs one would realise in the depths of one's mind and heart, that here is something closely connected with the Passion of Our Lord. Perhaps it is what the moderns call "atmosphere", or what the saints call "spiritual experience".

St. Paul's-Outside-The-Walls

A S it is one of the four major basilicas of Rome, it is
essential to know the basic facts concerning St. Paul's,
and a few of the immensely interesting minor facts.

It is wise for each pilgrim who is hoping to come to
Rome, to make a mental collection of a few pieces of
information about each of the places he intends to visit;
for, while on the spot, the wonders are so great and
unexpected and, in a word, so overwhelming, that there
seems to be no room for storing up facts. If they are
there beforehand, they will help vastly in one's power of
enjoyment of Roman experiences.

St. Paul's, therefore, was built over the burial-place of
the Apostle of the Gentiles. It was enlarged and beautified
in the course of the centuries; but in 1823 it was burnt
down, owing to the carelessness of a carpenter who was
repairing one of the beams in the roof and left a candle
burning too near the wood.

It was such a terrible disaster that the whole of Rome
was shocked by the news, which was kept from the Pope,
Pius VII (who had formerly been a monk at the Abbey
next to St. Paul's); he was dying already and it was
thought that the information would have killed him
immediately. However, the entire Christian world came
to the aid of the succeeding Popes in collecting funds
sufficient to rebuild it in all its glory. Fortunately the
great main arch which surmounts the high altar, and some
columns and statues were saved from the flames.

In our photograph of the exterior, the long body of the
basilica is seen to the right in the background, the foreground is occupied by the roof and windows of the transept,
together with a portico or vestibule. The great colonnaded
court which precedes the main entrance is not seen at all,
and that is well, for its exquisite beauty and majesty will

D

come as a surprise to the pilgrim. The bell-tower on the left is one of the least successful constructions erected after the fire.

The interior, of ancient classic design, is full of grace and dignity. Built originally (and restored in the same way) on the model of a five-aisle Roman basilica, it truly conveys the idea of being upheld by a forest of

The Basilica of St. Paul

columns. These magnificent pillars are reflected in the polished marble pavement as if in the calm waters of a lake. When you are there, remember to stand in a corner near the main door and to look at the columns diagonally; you will then see the truth of this comparison.

The papal altar is placed directly beneath the Gothic canopy, below the great arch which bears the weight of the roof. And, as the tomb of St. Peter lies directly below the canopy in the centre of St. Peter's, so directly beneath the altar under the canopy in St. Paul's lies a plain stone coffin or sarcophagus, with the inscription in Latin: PAUL APOSTLE. It is possible to obtain permission to venerate this sarcophagus, because the bronze grille which protects it can be opened. There lie the relics of the Apostle of the Gentiles, Saul of Tarsus, who met his Lord and Master on the road to Damascus over nineteen hundred years ago.

One of the most interesting features in St. Paul's is the series of circular portraits of the Popes, some of which are already familiar to us, beginning with St. Peter, and ending with several blank spaces in readiness for Popes yet to be. They were copied from sketches of the series as it appeared in the original basilica, and are generally accepted as authentic.

The windows are remarkable, as they recall the days when St. Paul's was first built, long before the use of glass for window panes had come into fashion. The marble tracery of the windows is filled in with thin slabs of transparent alabaster, which cast a mysterious golden light over the interior.

With regard to the four great Christian Powers in the middle ages which protected the four major basilicas, as already mentioned: Austria had St. Peter's under its special care; France, St. John Lateran; Spain, St. Mary Major and England, St. Paul's. English devotion to the great Saint is conspicuously shown by the erection of St. Paul's Cathedral in London, even if there were no other proof of the fact. The Kings of England are for this reason, in theory, honorary Canons of St. Paul's, and if today Queen Elizabeth were to visit the basilica (as Queen and not "incognito") she would be received in state by the Canons. Vestiges of the emblems of the Garter can be seen in some of the decorations there.

One should be on the alert not to miss the superb twelfth century cloister, built for the Benedictine monks, who have for centuries been in charge of St. Paul's. Happily it did not suffer in the fire of 1823, so the exquisite work of the famous "Roman marble-workers" may be seen still in all its glory.

There are many other things connected with this magnificent basilica which the pilgrim will find for himself—both new and old. Among the new, should be noted the main entrance-doors, designed and executed within the last twenty-five years, carried out in bronze, silver and enamel.

And among the old, there are the chains with which the Apostle was bound when he was in prison; they are quite authentic.

The Dedication of St. Peter's Basilica

NO other church in the world is like St. Peter's; that is a very obvious truth, of course, but it has, as it were, an extra claim to its unique quality in that it was dedicated twice, both dedications being celebrated on the same date: November 18th.

The first took place in the year 324 in presence of the Emperor Constantine, with Pope St. Sylvester officiating. The second took place on the same day of the month in 1626, just 1302 years afterwards, with Pope Urban VIII officiating, surrounded by twenty-two Cardinals.

In the old "Book of the Popes" it is narrated how Pope St. Anacletus buried the body of St. Peter near the Circus of Nero in the Vatican fields, and erected over it a small chapel or oratory, near which there soon came into being a cemetery, in which were buried the Popes who succeeded the Prince of the Apostles. This small chapel remained intact until the year 319, when, as Anastasius the Librarian tells us in his history, the Emperor Constantine, at the request of the Pope, built the basilica in honour of St. Peter.

The author of the "Book of the Popes" (which is our source for much of the history of the early Church) narrates how "in the days of Sylvester, Constantine Augustus raised to Blessed Peter a basilica close by the Temple of Apollo and decorated the sepulchre where the body of the Saint reposes".

When the foundations of the basilica were begun, we read in the same history that "having laid aside his crown and his imperial vesture, Constantine Augustus grasped a spade and began to dig the foundations of the church he intended to raise. Furthermore, on his own shoulders, he carried away from the place where he was digging, twelve heavy baskets of earth in honour of the twelve Apostles, thus imitating his ancestor of the Flavian family, the Emperor Vespasian who, when the Capitol was

The Tomb of St. Peter in the Vatican Basilica

destroyed by fire, himself dug the new foundations and carried away baskets of earth . . . ''

Constantine caused the oratory where lay the body of St. Peter to be lined with plates of bronze, and immediately above it built another chapel richly ornamented with gold and silver, sometimes called "the royal dwelling". Above this again, in the body of the church, was an altar with porphyry columns supporting a canopy. The top of the altar was of pure silver, framed in gold and enriched with sixty precious stones. In front of the tomb hung a golden candelabrum shaped like a crown, made of pure gold, weighing thirty-five pounds.

The Emperor also gave property in the East and in Egypt, the revenues of which were to provide oil for the many lamps that burnt near the tomb. The church was built in the form of a cross, "with a five-aisled nave and a magnificent atrium or vestibule and court". According to St. Gregory of Tours there were one hundred columns in St. Peter's and "many other beautiful things".

As the Emperor was anxious for the dedication to take place as soon as possible, the side walls of the Circus of Nero were used for the foundations of the left-hand aisles of the nave, and columns and marbles were taken hastily from pagan buildings and incorporated in the basilica. This use of the walls of Nero's Circus caused the sinking of the foundations in later centuries, and when the whole edifice threatened to collapse, Pope Julius II, in the sixteenth century, decided to re-build it in the form in which, more or less, we see it today.

This dedication of St. Peter's was the first to be carried out in any Christian church, hence its great importance, and hence the preserving of all details of the ceremony and the exact day of the month, for the second dedication in the seventeenth century. It has been remarked that the dedication of a church is in reality the burial of a martyr, even to this day, because the most important part of the ceremony consists in placing the relics of saints in the altar.

It is said that Constantine built seven churches in Rome. Moreover, when the exact origins of any very ancient Roman church cannot be easily traced, archaeologists generally solve the problem by saying "built by Constantine". It is certain that this great Emperor did much to encourage Christianity. If we are to believe the tradition regarding him, "after building these Roman churches he spent a year in Naples, accompanied by Pope St. Sylvester and there built seven more churches, after which he departed for the East to establish his empire at Constantinople". In Rome, a spot near the Aventine Hill is shown where "St. Sylvester and the Emperor Constantine embraced each other and parted forever".

As stated above, the foundation-stone of "new St. Peter's" was laid in 1506, because the walls of the older church had begun to crack and were, in some places, three feet out of the perpendicular. Besides this, the roof threatened to fall, countless rats having made holes in the beams. For a hundred years the work of rebuilding went forward in the midst of untold difficulties.

Some of these difficulties may be touched upon for the sake of illustration. In 1513, Julius II, who had begun the work, died; his architect, Bramante, died the following year. Leo X, who succeeded Julius II, entrusted the plans to Raphael, Sangallo and a Dominican friar; these three found that Bramante had built in too great haste and that the foundations required remodelling and strengthening. They also changed the plans. Then they died.

Peruzzi was called in by Leo X; he was a great architect with ideas of his own, so the plan was changed once more. In 1527, Rome was mercilessly sacked by Lutheran troops. Very little progress was made until 1546, when Pope Paul III summoned Michaelangelo, who was already in his 72nd year, to put his magnificent powers into the completion of the work. He died eighteen years later, but his superb plans for the dome were faithfully carried out by Giacomo della Porta.

In 1605, Pope Paul V again changed the ground plan, with Carlo Maderna as his designer, and finally the whole project was carried through. In 1626, the huge basilica, complete and in all its glory, was consecrated for the second time.

Our photograph shows the balustrade surrounding the sunken space in front of the Tomb of the Fisherman, with its ninety-three lamps which always burn there, as they did fifteen hundred years ago. And, be it remembered, this is the spot towards which millions of pilgrims have been converging from the ends of the earth, for nineteen centuries.

Michaelangelo's "Mother of Sorrows"

THE average pilgrim will not have a great deal of time to devote to viewing the artistic treasures of the Eternal City, except in so far as they are to be seen in the churches and basilicas. Fortunately a number of them are thus placed; and if one knows in advance what to look for and where, one can get an excellent first-hand knowledge of some of the stupendous achievements of those who painted, carved, and designed for the embellishment of Rome.

Therefore, we shall consider a work of art which all are bound to see, even if in Rome only for a few days.

Michaelangelo's Mother of Sorrows, or *Pietà* as the group is usually called, is placed over an altar in St. Peter's, on the same side as the Holy Door.

The famous author Pastor, in his "Lives of the Popes", wrote the following: "It is characteristic of the Eternal City that it possesses the power of attracting all that is prominent in the way of intellect, knowledge and art". This statement is true no less today than it was in the sixteenth century.

The hand that carved the *Pietà* was that of Michaelangelo Buonarroti, a Florentine, one of the greatest geniuses the world has ever known, equally powerful as an architect, a painter and a sculptor. To his mighty mind we owe the design of the dome of St. Peter's as it stands today. That was his masterpiece as an architect. As a painter he frescoed the famous ceiling of the Sistine Chapel, and as a sculptor he executed a number of superb statues, the finest of which is the *Pietà* in St. Peter's.

He was also a poet, and was employed successfully in the construction of fortifications and other military works.

He was born in 1474 and died in 1564, and what-ever he touched bore the imprint of genius. He always maintained that as his foster-mother was the wife of a

Michaelangelo's "Mother of Sorrows"

stone-cutter, from her he received his extraordinary facility in expressing himself in stone and marble.

At the age of twenty Michaelangelo came to Rome from Florence. There the French Cardinal, Jean Billiers de Groslaye, having seen some of the work done previously by the young sculptor, ordered him to carve a statue of

Our Lady of Sorrows for the French Chapel in St. Peter's, and offered him a block of perfect Carrara marble, together with 450 golden ducats.

The young artist began his masterpiece in the August of 1498, his mind still full of the grief caused by the death of his beloved mother and by the execution of the Dominican friar, Savonarola, for whom he had the greatest veneration. In the year 1500, in honour of the Jubilee, he completed the group which was solemnly placed in St. Peter's.

Such was the astonished admiration aroused by the *Pietà*, and such the incredulity expressed by many as to its authorship, that one night the young sculptor entered St. Peter's, and, by the light of a flickering taper, inscribed his name on the band that crosses Our Lady's breast. It was the only one of his works which he signed.

In the *Pietà*, Michaelangelo surpassed the achievements of the great sculptors who had preceded him, and outdid men of renown such as Donatello, Ghiberti, Jacopo della Quercia and Verrocchio.

The group represents a turning-point in the history of art, because although the figure of Our Lady is still akin to Florentine ideals (as seen especially in the treatment of her drapery), the figure of her divine Son is truly "universal", and belongs to no particular school of art. It is the representation of Him Who was the "most beautiful among the sons of men", not yet rigid, but at the actual moment of death, gently lying on His Mother's knees, as if one with her.

It would seem as if life were still in that divine Body; it is the graphic illustration of the fact that death could not triumph over God made Man. "O death, where is thy victory" is spoken by every line and feature of Our Lord's figure.

The calm peaceful expression of grief on the Mother's face does not diminish her youthful beauty. Her drapery lies in soft folds under the body of the Saviour, as if real.

The details of the group could be studied indefinitely, such as, for example, the rendering of Our Lord's right hand, the fingers of which almost clasp a fold of the Mother's mantle. Never before had the human form been represented in marble with such gentle realism, such grace and such profound reverence as in this marvellous group.

In its present position the *Pietà* is in a good light; but, it has been pointed out that it should be placed lower for its full effect to be obtained. However that may be, certainly it is placed where it may easily be found by pilgrims to St. Peter's, and so much of its loveliness can be appreciated as it is, that one hopes that no change will ever be made in its position or setting.

St. Peter's Colonnade

THE subject of St. Peter's colonnade is fascinating, and one is reluctant to leave it. There is so much to be said about it that would be found in no guide-book, that it is impossible not to make a few comments.

It is, in reality, a long curved portico, in the purest Doric style, about 45 feet wide. This space is divided into three aisles by four rows of columns. The middle aisle was intended for coaches, and is wide enough for two large ones to pass each other in comfort. The sides were meant for pedestrians. Carriages or motors are never allowed there at present, and foot-passengers have it all their own way.

Looking at the colonnade diagonally, as in our photograph on page 59, one can understand how the effect is said to be that of a forest of columns, as in the interior of St. Paul's-Outside-the-Walls. The women and children seated on the bases, give a good idea of the magnificent proportions of Bernini's masterpiece. It seems as if he had provided those seats on purpose. Perhaps that is why St. Peter's Square is sometimes called "the Roman's drawing-room". Any afternoon you may see young and old sitting at the foot of those majestic pillars, basking, in winter, in the warmth of the sun which strikes the eastern side; and, in summer, enjoying the cool shadow of the western side. It is the anteroom or vestibule of their Father's house and they are entirely at home.

So much for the forest of columns; but there is more to come. If you go and stand on a spot near the fountain, marked by a small disc of grey marble, you will behold the solution of one of the most difficult problems in architectural mathematics, for you will see what appears to be a row of single columns. One realises the power of the genius who designed this superb portico when remembering that it is curved. To the right, are seen the beautiful lines of the fountain, its windblown jet of water casting spray across the *piazza,* which, forming a pool, reflects the columns.

Much may be learned from the statues of the saints

The "forest of columns"

surmounting the columns, giving life and animation to the severely classic balustrade. There are 140 of them in all. Some are well known, like St. Sebastian or St. Francis Xavier; but some are quite unfamiliar like the actor St. Genesius who was ridiculing the Christians in a play, and suddenly, in presence of the pagan emperor, threw off his mask and his trappings, declared himself a Christian, and suffered a cruel martyrdom for his Faith.

His statue is the 42nd in line, and close to the entrance to the Vatican.   If you have any actor friends, bring your camera and secure a photograph of St. Genesius for them.

An amusing story is connected with our photograph below. The photographer, who was making a special study

"Human interest" in a study of light and shade

of light and shade, was intently busy with preparations to take the exquisite interior curve of the colonnade, showing the play of sunlight and shadow on rounded travertine and pavement which offer such a perfect example of rhythm in architecture.   At the crucial moment, four jolly little Roman urchins, tired of splashing about near the fountain, and on the lookout for adventures, decided that here was an ideal opportunity of getting themselves snapped, and of spoiling a classic study of the colonnade. Somehow, they seemed even more keen on the latter aim; and conveyed the impression that it was glorious fun to smash up a dull picture. Well, of course, they provided exactly what was wanted, human interest and perspective. And certainly, a good time was had by all.

In the anxious and dark days when Rome was bombed, 1943-44, the people of the city took refuge in the colonnade. They felt that no harm would come to them if they were close to the Tomb of the Apostle and to the person of the Vicar of Christ on earth. So they used to establish themselves there, safe from storm and from danger, pathetically trusting that all would be well. They used to bring their families, with blankets and provisions and everything needed for a prolonged stay. Many of them were unable to procure any provisions, for Rome was perilously close to famine. Like his Divine Master, the Pope had pity on the multitude and sent detachments of Catholic Action men and boys, with baskets of food for his hungry children in the colonnade.

The Triple Crown

THE solemn commemoration of the Holy Father's coronation is always held with full ceremonial on the anniversary of the event.

Of all great ecclesiastical ceremonies, the crowning of the Sovereign Pontiff is probably the greatest and most impressive. In the middle ages the name "Coronation Feast" was used for those high holidays on which the Pope wore his crown instead of a mitre. They were: Easter Sunday and Monday, Ascension Thursday, Whit-Sunday, St. Peter's Day, Christmas Day, St. Stephen's Day, Twelfth Night (i.e., the Epiphany) and the anniversary of his coronation.

Some of the striking features of the coronation ceremony are known to all, especially the dramatic moment when the pontifical procession halts on its way to the papal altar. A prelate advances towards the Pope bearing a wand topped by a wisp of flaming tow, which blazes up and then rapidly falls into ashes, while he intones the words: *"Sic transit gloria mundi"*—"Thus passes the glory of the world".

Probably less generally known, is the origin of the Triple Crown which is placed on the Pope's head by the Cardinal Deacon and which he always wears on solemn occasions. In the first place, the Pope is the only Sovereign in the world who wears one. Other crowns are of different shapes, this one is unique. Originally it was an Oriental mitre, somewhat resembling those worn by the Kings of Persia, of Phrygia, and of Parthia. Among the Jews it was worn exclusively by the High Priest, but it was forked in shape.

The first pontifical crown was probably a tall cone-shaped cap. In the thirteenth century it was ornamented by the three crowns—before that period there was only one crown at the base of the cap. In the centuries that followed the triple diadem became more ornate, and richer materials were used; jewels were added in varying numbers and the craftsmanship of the pontifical goldsmiths was said to surpass all others.

Several historical Triple Crowns are preserved in the

His Holiness Pope Pius XII giving his blessing for the first time after his coronation

treasury of St. Peter's and of the Sistine Chapel. During the Napoleonic occupation of Rome, when practically everything that could be looted was taken by the soldiers, including the papal tiara, Pope Pius VII was obliged to use one made of paper and cardboard, ornamented with imitation jewels, because in some ceremonies it was absolutely necessary for him to wear it.

At times of coronation anniversaries, when the papacy, as such, provides interest both for the faithful and for non-Catholics, reference is sure to be made to the famous old "Prophecy of St. Malachy".

St. Malachy was born at Armagh in 1094, was ordained a priest, and consecrated Archbishop of Armagh. In 1135 he set out on a journey to Rome and on the way stopped for some time at Clairvaux to visit his friend St. Bernard. It was as a result of this friendship, that on his return to Ireland he founded the first Cistercian monastery in that country, at Mellifont. On a second journey to Rome, he died in St. Bernard's arms at Clairvaux, in 1148.

He was the first Irishman to be formally canonised; an event which took place in 1190. The best authorities, in writing about St. Malachy, tell us that the "prophecies" found in Rome in 1590, and attributed to him were definitely not written by him.

However, their popularity has been widespread and, accurate or not, they are frequently mentioned and some means or other is found for interpreting them in the light of each pontificate. Thus the prophecy concerning Pope Urban VIII's "lilies and roses" was justified by the fact that his family coat of arms (that of the Barberini) showed bees among lilies and roses.

The last portion of the "prophecy" reads as follows:

"Flower of all flowers. From the half-moon. From the strength of the sun. Glory of the olive. During the final persecution of the Church, Pope Peter II will reign, he will feed his flock among many tribulations, and when they are over, the City of the Seven Hills will be destroyed, and the Great Judge will judge His people. Hence all will understand that the end of the world is near . . ."

We have quoted this from the *Osservatore Romano* and add the lines which conclude the article: "From the above it can be seen how fantastic, futile and irreverent these so-called prophecies are. It seems that their author was one Alphonsus Ceccarelli, an obscure sixteenth century writer. Whoever he may have been, both the author and his book are blameworthy and reprehensible. The future is in the hands of God, Who guides and directs human events for the greater good of mankind and for His everlasting glory.''

We have quoted the authoritative Vatican publication expressly, to vindicate a great Saint and a great Irishman from the accusation of having written these childish ''prophecies''.

The Vatican Museums

THERE are no museums in the world to compare with the Vatican Museums. It is noteworthy that, unlike all other great places of the kind, they have an "s" in their title. For we speak of the British Museum in London, the National Museum of the Louvre in Paris, the Metropolitan Museum in New York. Here, however, there is a whole series of them under one vast roof, representing world-scholarship, art, sculpture, architecture and learning of all kinds. Connected with them is the immense Vatican Library.

Like all buildings for the use of civilised man, they must be cleaned and overhauled periodically, and, in this case, the work is done in the summer. This is well for us, if we are here at that time, for we shall have the place to ourselves and shall not have to wait (as sometimes occurs) to take our turn to stand in a favourable position for viewing some masterpiece. Nor shall we be interrupted in our own quiet comments on the wonders lying before us, by the eager voices of lecturers and guides explaining things in their own way to their own groups.

This overhauling and cleaning does not involve any great moving or covering-up process, so we shall have nothing to lose and everything to gain by being there in the summer months. The wisest of the people who give advice to visitors in Rome, tell them to visit one section of the Vatican Museums, and then to take a day off in the neighbouring townlets and villages, to return again, and then to leave an interval once more. There is so much beauty, so much to wonder at and admire that the mind must necessarily rest in between visits.

The new entrance to the Museums was opened in 1932 by the late Pope Pius XI, who was, among many other things, a scholar and an accomplished art critic. The wide door is seen in our illustration, surmounted by the Pontifical coat-of-arms, flanked by heroic statues of Michaelangelo and Raphael as the dominating figures in Renaissance art.

The entrance to the Vatican Museums

Once inside, the arched entrance is seen in all its beauty. Against a background of grey-green marble rises an ascent forty-five feet in height copied from a similar one at Orvieto which bore the name of "St. Patrick's Pit". The one at Orvieto was constructed according to the description given in a medieval legend which related how St. Patrick saw the souls in purgatory both ascending and descending without ever meeting. The secret of the construction lies simply in there being two inclined planes, one above the other, widening out towards the top, in such a way that the whole suggests a broad and shallow inverted funnel.

The holy souls went up and down in St. Patrick's vision; at Orvieto the besieged garrison of the fortress sent donkeys loaded with casks to the well at the bottom of the pit to fetch water; but in the Vatican Museums visitors and scholars use the handsomely-decorated incline. All along the bronze balustrade are seen the arms of the Popes who developed the collections in the Museums.

In the sixteenth century, when admiration for all that was classic was awakening, a number of fine statues were found in excavations here and there in the city. They were brought to the successive Popes, who placed them in the gardens of the Vatican against a background of green foliage and ornamental buildings. Here their beauty was set off better than in any other way. They also stood in niches in great courts and near broad flights of steps. Thus, under Pope Julius II, was begun the collection that has never been fully completed and probably will continue to grow as the years pass.

Having ascended the slope of "St. Patrick's Pit" the visitor reaches the wide corridor that leads to the statuary. On his way he passes a branch of the Vatican post office, where the stamps of many varieties issued by the Governor of the Vatican City would fill the heart of a collector with envy. It is hard to pass by without sending at least a brief message home, to say where we are and in what august surroundings we are writing.

Greece and ancient Rome seem to live again in the statues and portrait heads that surround us as we enter the gallery of statues. Grace and purity of line are seen in the Greek figures; character and temperament in the faces of the Roman Emperors. Never before in history had strength, obstinacy, self-indulgence, pride or self-control been expressed in marble as by those Roman sculptors in their rendering of human features.

Farther on is a section known as the "Hall of the Animals" where every fantasy of classic imagination connected with animal life is given full play: stags, dogs,

The doorway leading to "St. Patrick's Pit"

panthers, a bull, are there engaged in all kinds of activities. An exquisitely graceful fawn stands not far from a most lifelike lobster, executed in dark green marble.   Many of these figures of animals, as well as those of deities, ornamented the gardens of rich Romans under the Empire.

One of the most remarkable objects in this collection of sculpture is a perfect model of a Roman chariot drawn by two prancing steeds, the whole carried out in white marble and a little less than life-size. Its value is twofold, first, on account of its unusual beauty and charm, secondly, on account of the knowledge it provides of the exact manner in which a Roman racing-chariot was built, together with details of the method of yoking the horses. The body of the chariot, in which the driver stood upright, was used during the Middle Ages as a Bishop's throne in the church dedicated to St. Mark. The carvings on it were, however, not suitable for an episcopal chair, and another throne was provided for St. Mark's, while the little marble chariot was taken to the Vatican.

Among the finest examples of pagan sarcophagi, or marble coffins, of which there are a large number, are those of children. Many of them bear reliefs of children playing games, throwing nuts down from trees, running after each other, riding goats or dogs or dolphins as if they were horses, pursuing rabbits, playing at keeping shop, driving lions yoked to a tiny chariot; in a word, carrying on playful activities with which childen all over the world and in all ages are associated. And those innocents, who died so long ago, are surely still playing in the heavenly fields, in the sight of the Divine Child Himself.

Restoring the Vatican Treasures

MUCH of the damage done by time, to the treasures of art in the Vatican City has been repaired by experts, working in the Vatican Laboratory for Restorations.

This laboratory or workshop was founded by the late Pope Pius XI solely for the preservation of the treasures housed in the Vatican Palace and Museums. Happily the damage was not due to war, but merely to the passing of time and to natural causes. The collapse of an entire wing of the Library in 1931, was one of the worst accidents which has ever occurred in the Vatican, but the valuable documents and frescoes which suffered on that occasion have been magnificently restored.

What concerns us more closely is the work done on Raphael's masterpiece of decoration in the apartments of Pope Julius II, which is known in the catalogues as "The Dispute Concerning the Blessed Sacrament". "Dispute" is wrongly used, being a careless translation from the Latin; the word should rather be the "Glorification" or "Apotheosis" of the Blessed Sacrament.

The great fresco is divided into three sections. Highest of all appears God the Father surrounded by golden rays of light and by angels. Beneath His throne is seen Jesus Christ, the Second Person of the Blessed Trinity, flanked by His Mother, and by His Precursor, St. John the Baptist. At either side of this central group is a row of saints and figures from the Old Testament.

Thus, to the left of the picture, at the end of the row, is St. Peter, holding the Keys in his hand and looking towards Adam his neighbour; next to Adam is St. John the Evangelist, writing his Gospel; and beside him King David with his crown and harp; the last two are St. Lawrence, Deacon and Martyr, and Jeremias the Prophet.

Starting from the opposite end we see, corresponding to St. Peter: St. Paul, bearing his sword; Abraham; St.

James the Greater; Moses with the Tables of the Law;
St. Stephen with the palm of martyrdom; and finally,
almost hidden by the clouds of glory surrounding the
Throne, Judas Macchabaeus, wearing a plumed helmet.

Lower, and immediately beneath the figure of the Risen

Raphael's great fresco of the Blessed Sacrament

Christ, is a Dove in a circle of light, symbolising the Holy
Ghost, surrounded by angels. Thus we have, in a straight
line, beginning at the top, God the Father, the Risen
Christ, the Holy Ghost, and on the altar beneath, the
Blessed Sacrament. The whole idea of this wonderful
fresco falls into a well-thought-out pattern if each detail is
considered with care.

The third division represents the earth, showing Saints

and Doctors who glorified the Blessed Sacrament most specially by their words and writings. The groups centre round the monstance containing the Blessed Sacrament, placed on a marble altar.

Among those drawing our attention to this centre, or lost in prayer, are St. Gregory the Great, St. Jerome (with his lion at his feet), St. Ambrose, St. Augustine, St. Thomas Aquinas, St. Bonaventure, Dante, and others too numerous to mention and difficult to identify.

There are several portraits in the groups: the young man in the foreground, pointing with his right hand to the altar, is said to be Raphael himself. Beyond him is an old man, supposed to represent Bramante, the first architect of "new" St. Peter's (which is dimly seen among the trees in the background). Sad to say, being a Florentine, he did not understand the peculiarities of the Roman subsoil, and the defective foundation he laid for that part of the Vatican which housed the Library sank with the passing of the centuries, and caused the tragic collapse of the "Sistine Wing" in 1931.

The great "Apotheosis" of the Blessed Sacrament was restored by a group of artists whose talent bordered on genius. Above all their slogan was "no faking". No touching-up or "finishing" was allowed, except where absolutely necessary for the clearer understanding of the artist's aim. In this process of restoration, before remedies were applied, the kind and the extent of the damage were ascertained by means of chemical analyses and ultra-violet rays. Cracks in the surface plaster provided the most serious problem. They were remedied in a truly ingenious manner. A long hollow needle, somewhat like a knitting needle with a hole near the point, and a syringe at the other end (on the lines of an ordinary hypodermic syringe) was used to inject liquid and very fine adhesive cement in the wall behind the crack. When this liquid dried it had the effect of pulling the edges of the crack together without the surface having been in any way affected.

Damage done by damp is remedied by the use of electric heat applied also from the rear. Small portions of plaster which may have fallen are replaced and coloured with the help of chemical analysis of the surrounding material.

The cracks in the "Apotheosis of the Blessed Sacrament" had first been noticed in 1896; subsequent examinations were made in 1924, 1930, 1934 and 1943. The last investigations showed that increasingly rapid deterioration of the surface allowed of no delay. Hence the far-reaching work undertaken to prevent any further decay.

The Sistine Chapel

A^T the beginning of November, once the Feast of All
Saints is over, many Masses are said in Rome for the
repose of the souls of the dead. Italians have a special
devotion to the Holy Souls and during their month they
remember them fervently.

The Holy Father himself is present at a Solemn Requiem
for the souls of all the Cardinals deceased during the
preceding year. The ceremony takes place in the Sistine
Chapel, so called because it was built in the fifteenth
century by Pope Sixtus IV. According to many experts,
the Sistine is the finest "chapel" in the world. It is really
a small church, and is of immense importance on account
of its magnificent decorations. It is therefore fitting that
it should be the scene of all smaller and more "reserved"
Pontifical functions, as well as the place chosen for the
election of a Pope when a Conclave meets.

Its plan and proportions are seen in the accompanying
photograph. The rich pavement in the foreground was
executed by the famous family called the "Cosmati" or the
"Roman Marble-Workers", because of the many pavements, Paschal candlesticks, altar canopies and even
cloisters which they constructed and decorated with a ribbon
pattern of brightly-coloured marble mosaic. The whole
effect of their pavements was that of a sumptuous Persian
carpet.

The delicately carved screen which divides the chapel
into two parts, was intended to indicate that the general
public should remain outside of the upper portion of the
chapel while the Pope was officiating. Inside the screen
are places for cardinals, bishops and prelates, as well as for
ambassadors and other important personages. The altar

is seen through the door of the screen, with the singing-gallery on the right. The Holy Father's throne is placed near the altar, on the side opposite to the singing-gallery.

The Sistine Choir is one of the finest in the world, and is quite apart from the choir of St. Peter's; each has its own singers and Master, and they never take part in the same ceremonies.

From the windows high up in the walls, shafts of light stream down on the worshippers below and illuminate the decoration of the walls and ceiling.

The Sistine Chapel

Originally, when it was finished in 1483, the ceiling was of deep blue ornamented with golden stars. The decoration of the walls was divided into three parts: between the windows were portraits of the Popes; the lowest part was painted in imitation of gold brocade hangings, while between the two was a series of great frescoes showing scenes from the life of Moses on the left, and from the life of Christ on the right.

Twenty-five years after the completion of these frescoes, Pope Julius II summoned Michaelangelo to redecorate the ceiling. Dismayed at the magnitude of the task before him, unable on account of his irascibility to work with assistants, the Master nevertheless caused a scaffolding to be erected immediately beneath the ceiling, and set to work, with no companion except one man to mix his colours. He did most of the painting lying on his back.

In two years, all but two months, the central portion was completed; it was an overwhelming achievement of human genius. Two years more passed, and in October, 1512, at last, the whole scaffolding was removed and the entire work revealed, to the immense satisfaction of Pope Julius II, and to the astounded admiration of the multitudes who flocked to behold it.

Apart from admiration for the powerful imagination which conceived the huge design, one is amazed by the mere labour involved in covering single-handed, under most fatiguing conditions, 10,000 square feet of ceiling, containing nearly three hundred and fifty figures in every conceivable attitude, many of them three times larger than life, yet finished with the utmost exactitude, down to the smallest details.

To summarise the work of the Master, one can say that here, framed in an elaborate architectural setting, the history of the creation is unfolded. There are nine rectangular spaces, alternately large and small, in which the following biblical scenes are represented: God creating light; God creating the sun, moon and plants on the earth; God creating birds and fishes; God creating man; the creation of Eve; the Fall; the Flood; Noah. The Creation of Man is considered to be the most striking of the whole superb series.

Twenty-five years later, Michaelangelo decorated the end wall of the chapel with a vivid representation of the Last

F

Judgment.   Our Lord as Judge appears in the centre, with
Our Lady, and the Apostles Peter and Paul nearby.   The
whole scene may be taken as an illustration of the words
of the *Dies Irae,* with terror, menace and despair as its
keynotes.   In the lower part of the composition the graves
give up their dead in answer to the fearful summons of the
trumpets; some of the damned struggle against their doom,
while others are dragged helplessly downward.   Though
showing Michaelangelo's unparalleled power in drawing the
human figure, the scene is unrelievedly pessimistic, and too
much emphasis is placed on the lost souls.   For, after all,
on the Day of Judgment many will be saved through the
Blood of Christ, shed when Mass is offered, as it is on the
altar which stands at the base of this terrifying work of
art.

The Papal Railway Station

THE capacious Vatican storehouses are replenished from a multitude of sources. But they are filled up only to be emptied with remarkable speed, because a very small proportion of what comes in to the Vatican City is used for local needs of the little State itself.

Thousands of tons of goods of every kind, particularly foodstuffs, are sent off throughout the length and breadth of Italy to relieve the needy and to be distributed by the parish authorities. The Holy Father is Head of the Universal Church and Patriarch of the West, but he is also Primate of Italy, and as such he is foremost in distributing food, clothing and medicines to his children. But other countries, particularly devastated Germany, also come in for a large share of his charities.

It was truly in the order of Divine Providence that the Lateran Treaty of 1929 provided for the construction of a special railway for the Vatican City. By means of this railway, supplies are brought directly thither without even the formality of passing through the Italian customs, therefore no duty is ever paid on them.

The railway line itself branches off from the station known as the "Rome-St. Peter's", about half a mile from Vatican City and after crossing a high viaduct, beneath which the Roman traffic passes undisturbed, it enters Vatican City territory and ends in a double line of tracks by the goods and passenger platforms.

The actual entrance for trains is composed of a wide archway closed by heavy bronze doors, as seen in the photograph. The doors slide forward in deep grooves and can be opened or shut in one minute by means of either electric or hand power.

The first time Pope Pius XI visited the station, when it

was completed, he exclaimed: "This is the finest railway station in the world!"

It is interesting architecturally, and presents moreover, some unique features. In the first place, though intended for important traffic, there is no ticket office, no bookstall,

Under the bridge and into the Vatican City Station

no restaurant and no left-luggage department. The reason for this is that it was intended primarily for the use of sovereigns and diplomats who might wish to reach the Vatican City without passing through Italian territory, and who would be received in state, and be lodged there during their visit.

The interior of the station consists of one great central hall flanked by two smaller ones, all three paved with polychrome marble and supported by handsome marble columns. A few marble urns and the Pontifical coat-of-arms supported by the symbolic figures of "Thought" and "Action" decorate this stately structure.

Outside, the wide *porte cochère* precedes the main entrance, which, in turn, is adorned by a fountain. At the end of each wing, on the façade, is an arresting bas-relief which stands out conspicuously against the restrained dignity of the rest of the building. They symbolise the oldest and the newest means of transport; that is, ships and airplanes, and are represented by the barque of Peter and the fiery chariot of the Prophet Elias.

The work involved in building the station and laying the tracks was not as simple as might appear at first sight, since the ground sloped sharply and important excavations proved necessary. A serious landslide which took place while the building operations were in progress, necessitated the removal of 47,000 cubic metres of earth and rock for the raiwlay cutting and embankment; of 74,000 cubic metres for the station itself, and of 33,000 for the approach to the station.

In all, 46,000 cubic metres of masonry were employed in the building, of which 2,660 were blocks of marble and travertine. Apart from the stone-carving and marble work on the interior, 142,500 working days were necessary for its completion.

However, when everything was finished, together with the expressed satisfaction of the Holy Father, the highest praise that was bestowed on the station and all its appurtenances was that it "appeared in no way unworthy" of the City to which it belonged.

Vatican Radio Station

THE recent improvements in the broadcasting station of the Vatican City are—to use an overworked word—spectacular. The original "Broadcasting House" built in the reign of the late Pope Pius XI having become quite inadequate, Pope Pius XII directed that the summer residence, built by Leo XIII on the highest point in the Vatican Gardens, should be enlarged, modernised, and turned into an up-to-date Radio Station.

On important occasions, no less than six operators are at work in the Control Room, transmitting (either directly, or linked up with other networks) to every part of the globe. Regular broadcasts are made in the following languages: English, Italian, French, Spanish, Polish, German, Hungarian, Czech, Portuguese, Russian, Ethiopian, Bulgarian, Latin, Lithuanian, Croat, Slovene, Dutch, Arabic, Ukrainian, Rumanian, Albanian, Latvian, Chinese, and occasionally in Japanese, Cingalese, Tamil, and various African dialects.

The central tower in this new station contains the chapel, the spiritual power-house for the world-wide apostolate of the spoken word. The keynote of the chapel is "supra-nationality", and illustrates the catholicity of the Church. The marbles in it are from all parts of the globe. The words inscribed on the frieze at the base of the dome which surmounts the chapel are Our Lord's words as given by St. Matthew: *"That which I tell you in the dark speak ye in the light: and that which you hear in the ear, preach ye on the housetops"*.

As well as broadcasts of a general nature, the radio station daily transmits the substance of sheaves of radio-grams which are sent thither by the officials of the Vatican post-office. At specified times the station is in communication with the great stations of the world. Thus, at midday, daily, the Vatican Radio is in direct communication with New York.

Moreover, a regular service for the benefit of the Secretariate of State is carried out continually. This service may be called "secret" as it is not known to the public in general. Shortly after the establishment of the

Operators at work in the Transmitting Room of the Vatican Radio Station

Vatican Radio, all Pontifical Nunciatures, Apostolic Delegations and Cardinals' residences were provided with powerful receiving sets, and a day and a time indicated for each of them to stand by for communications from the Secretary of State.

Naturally no absolutely secret information is conveyed in this manner, but orders are confirmed and directions given which otherwise would reach their destination much later if sent by letter or telegram. Thus, perhaps by letter to the Vatican an Apostolic Delegate may have described a possible undertaking, a scheme for the good of the country in which he resides, or have given the name of a candidate for an urgent appointment to some position in his department. At the fixed time, the Secretariate of State would broadcast to him: "We approve of the plan mentioned in your letter of such a date . . ." or else: "Your Excellency is requested to await the detailed instructions which will follow shortly".

The speech made by the Holy Father on the occasion of the opening of the station is one of the most eloquent ever pronounced, and because it is so little known we quote a portion of it: "To the whole created world. Being, through the secret designs of God Almighty, the successor of the Prince of the Apostles, of those whose words were to reach all peoples and all places, and moreover, being able, through this great invention, to speak to all men throughout the world, We speak in the words of Scripture: 'Hear O heavens and give ear . . . hear ye islands and ye the far-off people . . . let the whole earth listen to the words of my mouth . . . To God, Our first words are directed: glory be to God on high, and on earth peace to men of goodwill. Glory be to God who in our day, has given to men the power to cause their words to be heard at the ends of the earth; and may there be peace on earth where We represent the Divine Redeemer who came on earth proclaiming peace."

After giving glory to God, the Pope addressed himself to governments, to Bishops, to priests and missionaries, to Christians and to infidels, to rich and poor, to learned men and to workers, to victors and vanquished, to the suffering and the persecuted. His was the voice of an apostle, reaching to far places where no Christian voice had ever been heard before.

The greatest days for the Vatican Radio are those on which the Pope speaks personally, transmitting a speech for some special occasion such as a Eucharistic Congress. Then, too, the encyclicals are all broadcast, as well as requests for gifts for the missions; but the highest point of all is the broadcasting of a pontifical Mass in St. Peter's, when, during the solemn triple Elevation, the silver trumpets in the dome sound their poignantly sweet melody, and the silence of the kneeling throng in that vast basilica, is heard by the listener, if one can speak thus of hearing silence.

The polyglot staff of speakers at the Vatican Radio is composed largely of priests or religious who take regular turns at the microphone. One of the most interesting experiments carried out there was between Rome and Castelgandolfo by means of ultra-short-waves, when the entire staff gathered to hear the outcome. Needless to say it was ultra-satisfactory.

The way in which the huge pylons of the station dominate Rome, is symbolic of their power. There are, of course, several other important Roman stations, particularly those near St. Paul's-Outside-the-Walls, and on *Monte Mario,* near the little Observatory; but they are dwarfed by the gigantic Vatican installation.

During the war the messages from the Vatican were, of course, intercepted and recorded, but never once did any announcer give news or express opinions which would have stultified the results of his work in the service of the Holy Father and of suffering humanity. They were much too wise for that, and their wisdom was shown by the magnificent results they obtained as instruments of the Pope's charity.

The Pope's Fire Brigade

ST. ANTHONY ABBOT who died in his hermitage in
Egypt about sixteen hundred years ago, is the Patron
Saint of the Vatican Fire Brigade, and his feast is kept on
January 17th.

Why is he their patron? During his long and austere
hermit's life in the desert we are told that he was attacked
by temptations so severe that they resembled flames. In
the middle ages he was specially invoked against
erysipelas, a disease which was popularly known as "St.
Anthony's Fire". In art he is often shown with a small
flame in his hand. No one, therefore, could be more
appropriately chosen as the patron of firemen.

The Vatican Fire Brigade does not share the celebrity of
the more conspicuous Swiss and Noble Guards, but its
members are none the less important employees of the
Holy See.

They are called the *Vigiles* as were the ancient watch-
men in the days of the Roman Emperors, and indeed
not only do their duties include the extinguishing of
fires which may occur in the Vatican City, but they are
also summoned in any other emergency, such as floods,
accidents, collapse of buildings (as when a floor of the
Vatican library fell in some years ago) or in any case
whatever where strong arms and efficient workers are
needed.

During heavy rains, they may receive no less than 25
calls for assistance during one night, as many places can
be affected by the onrush of the water. They even go up
to the Vatican Radio Station to help to set the pumps to
work, lest the valuable apparatus be damaged by flood.

They are possessed of the most modern machinery for
extinguishing fires, as well as for rendering assistance of all
kinds. A truck with hook-and-ladder attachment, hose,

chemical extinguishers, megaphones, motor-cycles, every kind of fire-fighting contrivance is at their disposal and is housed in their station.

The Duty Room of Vatican City Fire Brigade

A man and an officer are always on duty to receive incoming calls. They are smartly equipped and smartly drilled and can compare favourably with any fire brigade in the world.

Among other aids to efficiency are five hundred hydrants scattered through the streets of the Vatican City and five hundred more located in the various buildings. There is certainly no lack of water at their disposal. The hydrants are continually inspected and maintained in working condition.

Among other duties entrusted to the Vatican Firemen is that of overlooking the general condition of the buildings in the City and of pointing out flaws in their construction which might lead to danger.

The fire station is located in the south-east wing of the palace looking onto the *Cortile del Belvedere,* underneath the Gallery of Inscriptions which forms part of the Vatican Museums. On the ground floor are kept the new fire engines, trucks, ladders, ropes, extinguishers, hoses, spotlights, and other apparatus, including the motor cycles already mentioned. On the floor above are the sleeping quarters, kitchen, dining-hall, tailoring department and infirmary.

Every afternoon one of the firemen together with a Pontifical Gendarme makes the rounds of all the buildings of the Vatican Museums, Galleries, Offices and Archives. This tour takes about two hours. Another task of theirs is that of watching continually in St. Peter's when the wooden tribunes have been erected for pontifical ceremonies such as beatifications and canonisations. Night and day they remain on duty until the last wooden partition has been removed. Their task is no sinecure.

The Feast of St. Anthony is kept enthusiastically. In the morning the entire Brigade, in dress uniform, marches to the church of St. Anne, where Mass is celebrated by the Archbishop Vicar for the Vatican City. Be it noted in passing, that the Pope, as Bishop of Rome, has a Cardinal Vicar for the City itself, and a specially nominated Vicar for the Vatican City, who is always an Augustinian.

At this Mass every man receives Holy Communion. Returning to their gaily-decorated quarters for breakfast, they make ready for the visit of the Cardinal, President of the Pontifical Commission for the Vatican City. His Eminence arrives about midday, accompanied by the State Councillor, and the Director of the Technical Services of the City. They are received in state by the Director of the Vatican Services, the Lieut.-Colonel of the Pontifical Gendarmes and by the officers and men of the brigade.

The Sergeant-Major then makes a speech of welcome in the name of all present, and the Cardinal usually answers reminding the members of the Brigade of the importance of their duties and making reference to the powerful protection of their great Patron, St. Anthony, who shields them not only from material dangers but also from temptation and spiritual dangers such as he met and overcame so valiantly long ago in the desert. After the Cardinal and his suite depart, officers and men gather in the mess-hall for a festal dinner. St. Anthony's statue is in their midst, surrounded with lights, garlands and flowers, and he seems to look on with delight at the celebrations held in his honour. It is said that the Vatican Fire Brigade has a very special place in his affections.

The Vatican's Daily Newspaper

THE *Osservatore Romano,* official organ of the Vatican City State, expresses the opinion of the Holy See unofficially, and sometimes officially. It is subject to guidance from the authorities but enjoys great freedom in many ways. And no serious student of contemporary international politics can afford to neglect reading it.

Its offices are in the Vatican City, at the end of a charming narrow street. When approaching one has the impression of entering a small and rather lonely road in an unimportant provincial town. But the impression soon fades when one passes the various storehouses, workshops, residences and the little church situated in it.

Finally one reaches the circulation offices of the *Osservatore* and beyond them the editorial department. Next to this are the stores, and farther on, the presses which you will probably find roaring at full speed. Not to enter into too many technicalities of the trade, suffice it to say that the machines are of the latest pattern and in perfect condition.

Next door to the offices is the press room for the use of journalists seeking information from authentic sources. This was opened under the direction of the Secretariate of State in order that clear and well-defined facts and statements should be available to those who sought them. Some journalists, however, preferred at the time of its opening, and later also, to rely on rumours, gossip, and "it is said in authoritative circles" for their Vatican news. Such news is always read with eager interest, even by the enemies of the Church. Why is it that anything headed "Vatican" is the most popular item in any paper in any language and in any place?

It would be well if the *Osservatore* were to come out in various overseas editions. This was attempted at one time in South America, but the well-worn phrase "technical difficulties" covered the retreat of the bold spirits who made the endeavour.

The paper defines itself as "a daily politico-religious journal" and prints the Triple Crown and Keys on its masthead. It is dated "Vatican City" but provides facilities

The offices of "Osservatore Romano" are "at the end of a charming narrow street"

in Rome as well as in the Vatican City for publicity and distribution.

The first column on the front pages is headed "Our Information" and invariably begins with the list of audiences. private, semi-public and public granted by His Holiness. This is followed by official notifications inserted by the Prefect of Pontifical Ceremonies of coming events such as Consistories, Beatifications, Masses for deceased Cardinals, and similar functions.

If the Holy Father has made an important speech or issued an Encyclical then the front page is entirely given over to it. Otherwise events of world importance are discussed in paragraphs of varying length, and the concerns of one country or series of events are dealt with in two columns entitled *"Acta Diurna"*.

Once a week a page is devoted to accounts of religious activities or to the political activities of Catholics in other continents. The achievements of English Catholics come in for the lion's share of this section and lengthy quotations are often made from the Catholic press. To choose some of the items at random in recent copies of the *Osservatore* there appear the following: "Priests in China", "The Five-Year-Plan in Spanish Morocco", "Portuguese Colonisation in India", "The Economic Situation in Switzerland", "Native Administration in South Africa", "Catholic Action in Ireland".

The illustrations in the *Osservatore* are remarkably good, considering the quality of the paper, which, in common with all other dailies, it is obliged to use. Two photographers are accredited to it: Felici and Giordani; the former specialises in groups and events, the latter in views and impressions. At great functions in the Vatican Basilica they join forces and share in photographing the vast expanse of the church with its congregation of sixty-thousand people.

The paper originated on July 26th, 1860, when the Deputy Home Secretary of the Pontifical States, Marcantonio Pacelli, a member of the family of Pope Pius XII, gave permission for its publication. Its vicissitudes were many. Two printers were found who, by means of old-fashioned presses produced at first thirty copies an hour. Next came a larger press which could print 1,000 copies in the same length of time.

Progress was made when the editor undertook to print

the telegrams with the news of the Franco-Prussian War of 1870. Circulation rose by leaps and bounds, and two editions were issued, a morning and an evening one. At present it is exclusively an evening paper.

After the fall of Rome in 1871 it continued publication, unhindered by the Italian King and Parliament. In fact every event of importance in the history of the Church was chronicled at length and with unimpeachable accuracy in its columns. The epoch-making Encyclical *Rerum Novarum* appeared first in its pages.

In 1929 it transferred its offices and presses to special precincts in the Vatican City, thereby becoming, as mentioned above, the organ of the Vatican City State.

The words written in the first issue of the paper find an echo in the latest. They were its dedication: "We (the editors and publishers) place at the august feet of His Holiness this undertaking, begging his blessing, in which we shall find our strength and our encouragement."

Needless to say the Holy Father takes an active interest in the *Osservatore;* it is the first of the newspapers that he reads daily in the course of his work.

G

In the Vatican Gardens

FROM August 15th to October 15th the inhabitants of the Vatican City are theoretically "on holiday". It seems strange that their vacation should take place so late, but the truth is that September and October are the ideal months in which to leave Rome and pay a visit to the neighbouring *Castelli Romani* or even to go farther afield. And the benefit of such a holiday is felt more in the months of hard work during the winter. Still, it does strike a northerner as an out-of-the-way custom.

Whilst those who can do so leave Rome for at least a short time, others make use of their privilege of frequenting the Vatican gardens.

Although not in any way large, compared to some other parks and estates, the Vatican gardens offer such a variety of views and of cultivation that they convey an impression of much larger extent than they really possess. Our photograph shows something of this. It depicts a mysterious fountain trickling among the rocks in a shadowy glade, which might be far distant from any city. Many portions of them recall the elaborate Renaissance Italian gardens.

On entering, we follow a wide road flanked by lemon trees growing in enormous terra-cotta pots. The road leads to a little wooded height in the centre of which is a shrine of Our Lady of the Guard, dedicated to her under the name because it is that under which she watches over the port of Genoa; and Pope Benedict XV, during whose pontificate the shrine was erected, was a native of Genoa. The shrine itself was a gift of the Genoese.

Perhaps of all Popes of this century Benedict XV made most use of the gardens. He drove out in them at the customary time in the afternoon, accompanied, as usual, by one of his Domestic Prelates.   But besides these "official" outings he often slipped away there by himself or with only one companion, immediately after his midday meal.

A secluded fountain in the peace of the Vatican Gardens

One hot afternoon, together with his secretary, he passed from his own apartments, through the Museums and out to the gardens.   However, the great gates at the entrance were locked and the *gendarme* on duty was sound asleep. Aroused by the secretary, the man's dismay can easily be imagined when he discovered that the Pope himself was waiting for the gate to be opened.

Another story is told of Benedict XV making his way towards the gardens by the front entrance of the Vatican

Museums. Now this particular entrance possesses a turnstile so that the number of persons having bought tickets of admittance to the Museums may easily and accurately be counted. The gatekeeper was nonplussed on seeing His Holiness and a Domestic Chamberlain waiting at the turnstile. Was he to take the responsibility of letting them in free, and so upsetting the calculations of the day's receipts, or—what? The Pope, however, solved his difficulty by pulling out a purse and giving him several coins. "Here," he said kindly, "pay for Monsignor and for me out of this, and keep the rest for yourself." So the Sovereign Pontiff paid admission to his own Museum and gardens.

Benedict XV not only used to go to pray at the shrine of Our Lady of the Guard, but he used to spend a few minutes first with some very special goldfish in one of the ponds, feeding them with very special biscuits which he crumbled with his own hands; then he would go on to two magnificent Indian parrots which he fed with almonds and walnuts.

The shrine of Our Lady of Lourdes at the top of a hill has been a favourite resort for the Popes since its erection by the French for Leo XIII. It is a realistic reproduction of the Rock of Massabielle, with a statue of Our Lady in the cleft where she appeared to Bernadette. An altar stands beneath the statue just as at Lourdes. Mass has frequently been said at this altar, either by the Popes themselves or by their delegates. Near the Grotto of Lourdes is the famous bronze statue of St. Austremon, Bishop of Auvergne, given for the Golden Jubilee of Pope Leo XIII by the Catholics of Auvergne.

Continuing on our way we come to the old Leonine Walls which bound the gardens. They were built by Pope St. Leo III, as a protection against the Moorish invasions, about the time that King Alfred was reigning in England. They give a touch of medieval picturesqueness to the landscape and provide a background for a charming house built by Leo XIII as a summer residence, now used as the Vatican Broadcasting Station.

Beyond this lie some open fields used for the cultivation of grapes and vegetables. Of late years the grapevines have been abolished, because some enterprising gardeners who were allowed to keep a certain quantity of the grapes for their own use made wine of them, bottled it and labelled it "The Pope's Wine". One can easily imagine why the Pontiff suppressed this particular branch of the wine trade when he heard about it.

The fountains in the Vatican gardens are celebrated for their variety and number. Our photograph shows a quiet, secluded fountain typical of the restfulness and peace of the woods. However, besides the smaller ones are the famous "Altar of the Blessed Sacrament", in which six upright jets represent candles, standing on either side of a circular spray, representing a monstrance. Then there is "The Galleon", which consists of a large model of a Spanish galleon in full sail with water spouting from the end of every mast, spar and gun, as well as the bowsprit. It is made of bronze and has been described as a very handsome and impressive toy. But it is more than that; it is really a work of art. Another fountain is dominated by a great stone eagle above a broad pool.

The "House of Pius IV", a beautiful example of an ornate early Renaissance building, where the Academy of Sciences now holds its meetings, is one of the glories of the gardens, standing as it does amid lawns, trees and shrubbery.

Shopping in the Vatican City

ONE generally associates the Vatican with magnificent tapestried halls paved with marble or mosaic and majestic sculptured archways. All those things are there, of course, but there is also a business quarter and a small shopping district.

They were organised and built after the Lateran Treaty in 1929, which gave the Vatican City international status, and created it a sovereign State, apart from the universal spiritual power of the Holy Father as Pope. The latter extends over the whole world; the former, that is to say, the Pope's power as temporal Sovereign of the Vatican City State, extends over a territory of about two square miles. Nevertheless he exercises a definite sovereignty and as Ruler he has entrusted the commercial side of the life of his State to a special commission of laymen headed by a Cardinal.

Among other advantages, goods entering the Vatican City are not in any way subject to Italian customs, therefore they are provided for the "citizens" at a lower price.

Our photograph shows the shop where provisions are sold. All foodstuffs are available. Each "citizen" of the Vatican State has his or her identity card or passport, so that no outsiders may avail themselves of privileges to which they have no right.

Prosaic hand-carts and delivery-tricycles come and go in front of the shop, which hums with activity from 7-30 a.m. until 11-30. It then closes for the day.

Housekeepers in the employ of prelates and officials of the Vatican arrive with bags and baskets, for fruit, vegetables, cheese, eggs, meat and wine.

Milk, vegetables, eggs and fruit come from the model farm situated in the pontifical villa at Castelgandolfo. It was bombed heavily during the war and the herd of Swiss cows had to be removed, but now, of course, it is in running order and those who have the privilege of buying the farm produce know that they are never overcharged and that they are getting wonderful value for their money.

Vatican City's Food Shop

Italian currency is used in the Vatican shops. It was found that the pontifical coinage was so eagerly snapped up by collectors that it went almost immediately out of circulation; by the terms of the Lateran Treaty both Italian and Vatican coinage were to be accepted in both States.

The Vatican has never issued paper money, but as most Italian currency is of paper the Vatican shops also use it.

The photographer responsible for our illustration was standing just in front of the Vatican pharmacy where medicines of all kinds are sold by the *Fatebenefratelli*. The name means literally "The Brothers Who do Good".

They are the hospitallers of St. John of God and manage a big hospital on the Island in the Tiber; for that reason the Holy Father appointed them chemists-in-ordinary to the Vatican.

In the background of the photograph, the rear wall of the Vatican post office is seen. There are several small post offices in the City but this is known as the "Central Post". From there letters may be sent to all parts of the world, as well as telegrams and radiograms.

The Dominicans

THE great Religious Orders have their strongholds in the Eternal City and every pilgrim will probably have a vital interest in one or other of them. Obviously no pilgrim would have time to visit the places connected with all the various Orders.

St. Dominic's Rome begins at the great church of *Santa Sabina* where he died in the year 1221, "in another Friar's cell and wearing another Friar's habit because he had none of his own", so runs the chronicle. One of the treasures of *Santa Sabina* is the famous painting by Sassoferrato, representing Our Lady giving the rosary to St. Dominic and St. Catherine of Siena.

There are countless copies of this beautiful and touching picture in existence, and it is not generally known that this one is the original. Certainly it is a masterpiece. Our Lady is seen seated on a carved throne of dark wood bearing the Holy Child on her knee. On her right kneels St. Dominic, his youthful face lit by an ecstasy of wondering love as he receives the rosary from her. On her left, St. Catherine with bowed head, her face in the shadow of her coif and veil, receives from the Holy Child, both a crown of thorns and a rosary. Lilies and roses lie at Our Lady's feet between the two Saints, while baby cherubs hover exultingly above the throne. Throughout Christendom this is the picture generally recognised as *the* "Our Lady of the Rosary".

From *Santa Sabina* we may go to the next largest and most important Dominican centre in Rome. It is the celebrated *Collegium Angelicum,* one of the Pontifical Universities, which maintains a staff of Dominican professors, specialists in all branches of theology and philosophy, and which is empowered to grant theological Degrees.

Its undergraduates include not only Dominicans (who come from all parts of the world, making it a truly "International College") but members of other Orders, and candidates for the diocesan clergy.   The church next to it,

"Our Lady of the Rosary" by Sassoferrato in the
ancient Dominican Church of St. Sabina

a beautiful example of late Renaissance architecture, is dedicated to SS. Dominic and Sixtus.

The massive medieval walls of this stronghold of the "Watchdogs of the Lord" are completed by equally medieval towers, and the view from them which stretches out across ancient Rome is unique in the world. It includes the Roman Forum with its remains of ancient grandeur, the Palatine Hill where the Caesars had their luxurious dwellings, and the heights of the Janiculum, Rome's bulwark against the barbarians.

From the *Angelicum* we proceed to the church of the Minerva—its real name being *Santa Maria Sopra Minerva,* that is "Our Lady Above Minerva", because her church was built on the ruins of a temple to the Goddess of Wisdom. It would seem to be the heart of Dominican Rome, for memories of St. Catherine of Siena cluster thickly about its walls. Here she prayed, and suffered; the rooms she occupied when in Rome were situated close by, and her incorrupt body lies under the high altar.

Wonderful works of art are seen here also. One of the best known is the large chapel of St. Thomas Aquinas on the right of the high altar, completely decorated by the Florentine, Filippino Lippi. Then, too, the remains of the "Angelic Painter" the saintly Dominican, John of Fiesole, generally known as Fra Angelico, lie in a quiet tomb to the left of St. Catherine's resting-place. Five Popes are also buried there, and the vaulted cloister beside the church (to which pilgrims are fortunately allowed access) is a place in which to dream dreams and see visions of the Blackfriars who lived and prayed there throughout the centuries.

How we have lingered! We shall have to take one of those little one-horse victorias called *carrozzelle,* or else a prosaic taxi and speed over to *San Sisto Vecchio* ("St. Sixtus the Ancient") near the Baths of Caracalla. It is now occupied by Dominican nuns who take care of orphans, but it was built originally on the site where St. Lawrence met Pope St. Sixtus II, who was being carried off to martyrdom. His grief at not being allowed to accompany the beloved Pontiff has been beautifully described by St. Augustine and St. Ambrose.

In 1217, *San Sisto* was bestowed on St. Dominic personally by Pope Honorius III, and miracle after miracle

was wrought by the Saint within its walls.   Here it was
that two angels brought a meal for the brethren seated at
their bare tables, when all the food in the house had been
given to the poor.   Three times, on this spot, did St.
Dominic raise the dead to life.   These occurrences were
illustrated by Père Besson, a great French Dominican
artist, who lived in the last century, on the walls of the
Chapter House, now a chapel where Mass is said daily.

Then, we go back to the Irish Dominicans at St.
Clement's, whose church deserves a chapter to itself.

The Benedictines

DID you know that there are eight churches and monasteries in Rome closely connected with St. Benedict and his sons? Some are very old, one is very modern. We begin with the modern one.

Familiarly known as *Sant' Anselmo* it is officially "The International College of the Benedictine Order". Originally founded in 1687, as a place of studies for Benedictine monks from all parts of the world, it was closed in 1837, and re-established in 1887, by Pope Leo XIII.

He took a deep personal interest in the progress of the work, as it went forward under the capable guidance of the celebrated Abbot de Hemptinne. Today it rivals *Santa Sabina* as an outstanding building on the Aventine Hill.

From all the other hills of Rome *Sant' Anselmo* is seen dominating the height with its fine tower, and claustral buildings. The latter include several beautiful colonnaded cloisters. There is a unique feature in the church which never fails to interest pilgrims. In the pavement are outlined the Greek and the Roman letters which, in the form of a great X, are always traced in ashes by the Bishop during the solemn consecration of a church. Here the letters are permanent.

The singing is as it would be in any Benedictine monastery, superlatively good, and the services during Holy Week are thronged with visitors who want to hear "the best there is". If you expect to be in the Eternal City during Holy Week and you admire the Benedictine chant remember *Sant' Anselmo* on the Aventine.

The great major basilica of St. Paul's-Outside-the-Walls is under the care of the Cassinese Congregation of Benedictines, who have been there since the eighth century. Among the great ones who resided in the monastery adjoining the basilica are St. Odo of Cluny in the tenth century, and Hildebrand, later Pope St. Gregory VII, in the eleventh century, who was called from Cluny to Rome by the Pope, to be made Abbot of St. Paul's.

St. Gregory the Great celebrating Mass

The Benedictine spirit is strong in all that is connected with the abbey and the basilica, and the cloister is a place in which to dream of monastic peace and beauty.

Hidden away in the centre of Rome, near the Palace of the Massimo family and not as well known as it should be, are the church and the small monastery of St. Ambrose.

They are said to be built on the site of the Saint's family mansion. It is another Benedictine stronghold, for the monks have been there from time immemorial. And there is preserved one of the greatest treasures of the Order: an ancient fresco of Our Lady and the Holy Child, held to be the very picture before which St. Benedict prayed when he was a schoolboy in Rome, before his flight to the solitude of Subiaco.

Subiaco, of course, is a name to conjure with, although it is not actually in Rome, being a matter of 45 miles outside the city. No lover of the Saint should omit to visit the rocky solitude where the cave in which he lived is still in a state of perfect preservation, and the first of his monasteries, St. Scholastica's, opens hospitable arms to visitors and shows them all her treasures.

St. Benedict's own dwelling, that is his ancestral home, was situated in the *Trastavere* (or "the city across the Tiber"). A small church now stands on the spot and there we are shown the chapel in which he prayed and the room where he studied. The church with its charming little belfry was erected in the eleventh century; its bell is the oldest in Rome, bearing the date 1085.

St. Gregory's church and monastery, of course, next claim our attention, they are situated near the Colosseum and are very easy to find; English pilgrimages converge at *San Gregorio* as at their natural goal. From there St. Gregory the Great sent his monks to convert England, headed by St. Augustine of Canterbury. This is stated in a thrilling inscription in the cloister which enumerates the names of occupants of English Sees who set forth from St. Gregory's own house, transformed into a Benedictine monastery.

"St. Praxed's ever was the church for peace," wrote Robert Browning after his stay in Rome. It stands on the site of the house of Pudens, a Roman Senator and friend of St. Peter, and is therefore older than the Benedictine Order itself.

The treasures therein preserved are numerous, not least among them being the column of the Flagellation of Our Lord, brought back from the Holy Land by Cardinal Colonna, in the thirteenth century. Devotion keeps pace with the times, for although *Santa Prassede* possesses one of the most ancient apse-mosaics in the Eternal City, yet it also boasts of one of the most modern ones. In a side chapel, the semi-dome above the altar has recently been ornamented by a fine mosaic showing Our Blessed Lady in the centre, surmounted by a representation of the Blessed Trinity. On one side of Our Lady is a group of Benedictine monks headed by their Founder, and on the other a group of Benedictine nuns led by Saint Scholastica. There is no other mosaic of the kind to be compared with this one, both for beauty of conception and skill in execution.

The church of St. Frances of Rome, originally known as "St. Mary's the New" is served by the Olivetan Benedictines, that of *San Stefano del Cacco* by the Silvestrian Benedictines.

(*A full explanation of the picture of St. Gregory the Great celebrating Mass will be found on page* 134.)

The Jesuits

NUMBERS of pilgrims are linked to the Society of Jesus by ties of friendship or relationship, and access to the places of interest and devotion connected with St. Ignatius and his spiritual sons are made easy for them.

First and foremost is the church of the Holy Name, or as it is called in Italian the *Gesù*. It is sometimes called the "Mother Church of the Society", as it was built during the lifetime of St. Ignatius by his friend and admirer Cardinal Farnese who summoned the best architects in Rome, Vignola and Giacomo della Porta, to design it.

The interior is richly adorned with coloured marble and bronze. Its greatest treasure is, of course, the tomb of St. Ignatius, which is one of the important artistic features of Rome. The details of the bas-reliefs, statues and marbles that surround it provide a study in themselves. Some idea of the whole may be gained from our photograph.

In the sarcophagus beneath the altar lie the mortal remains of the Founder. In the transept opposite is preserved the arm of St. Francis Xavier, that strong right arm which, we are told, used to fall helpless from exhaustion after having baptised thousands of pagans in succession.

Next door to the *Gesù* is the building in which are the rooms occupied by St. Ignatius when he was General of the Society. They are small and cramped and up two flights of stairs. But what a reward when you reach them! If ever walls preserved the memory of the life of a Saint which pulsated within them, they are the walls of those rooms.

In one of them a mysterious little door opens upon an equally mysterious balcony. Here it was that Ignatius in the brief intervals in his work, used to step out for a

H

breath of air and a glance at the stars. And here, we are told, he sighed: "How dull are the things of earth when I behold the heavens!"

Various copies of letters hang on the walls, and not least

The greatest treasure of the "Gesu" is the tomb
of the founder, St. Ignatius

among them is one written by his own hand and bearing his seal and signature. The exquisitely clear and firm writing is just as it was when he gave it to the waiting messenger to be carried to its destination. It concerns windows in a building under construction, and has all the courtesy of Spain, as well as the clear-headed businesslike quality which distinguished his thought.

The *Gesù* is not far from the *Chiesa Nuova,* St. Philip Neri's church, also known as *Santa Maria in Vallicella* or "St. Mary's of the Little Valley". One can imagine the two Saints meeting each other in the narrow streets. We know that Philip always stopped "Father Ignatius" for a few words of spiritual intercourse when they met, and that buttons were lacking on the latter's cassock, owing to Philip Neri's habit of literally holding the Saint by a button during the conversation. He ran no risk of Ignatius' escaping from him.

Our Lady of the Wayside has her shrine in the *Gesù,* to the left of the High Altar, and the tiny chapel is never empty of devout clients who crowd there to beg her protection.

The church of *Sant' Ignazio* which is only five minutes' walk distant from the *Gesù,* was a gift to the Society from Cardinal Ludovisi in 1626, in honour of the canonisation of the Founder. The proportions are singularly noble, and the nave, with its glorious ceiling, is one of the finest architectural works of the seventeenth century.

In one transept lie the remains of the Saint of the princely House of Este, Aloysius Gonzaga, with the armorial bearings of his family on pillars and hangings. In the opposite transept, in a correspondingly beautiful altar-tomb, lie those of the little Belgian plebian Saint, John Berchmans. Both are identical except for the fact that where the former shows heraldic emblems, the latter is ornamented by the Holy Name on a shield. Not only death, but the Society of Jesus is a great leveller; high and low come to the service of the Master under the same conditions of humble obedience.

Behind *Sant' Ignazio* stands the Roman College, the first of the long line of Jesuit Colleges and schools, and the forerunner of the Gregorian University. The latter is now housed in an imposing modern building in *Piazza della Pilotta,* while the original Roman College building has been taken over by the Italian Government. However, on the top floor, the rooms occupied by St. Aloysius and St. John Berchmans remain the property of the Society of Jesus, and here again, the saintly lives lived there have left something unspeakably real and impressive in the atmosphere. In glass cases there are to be seen the note-books of both Saints; very neat and painstakaing are the pages of the geometry notes written by hand, illustrated by diagrams, and showing what a Renaissance Saint could achieve in the matter of secular knowledge. One could linger indefinitely over them, up in those wonderful rooms perched high above the roofs of Rome.

The present residence of the Father General is no longer at the *Gesù,* but in a spacious modern building close to the Vatican City—*Borgo Santo Spirito* 5, is the exact address—and one likes to think that there must be much more air and light there than in the old cramped quarters under the Capitoline Hill.

Nearly all the greater Roman churches enshrine memories of St. Ignatius and his followers. Most important of all is St. Mary Major where he said his first Mass on Christmas night at the altar of the Crib.

St. Stanislaus Kostka, whose radiant sanctity makes him in a special way the Patron of all novices, lies buried in *Sant' Andrea al Quirinale.* This church in *Via Venti Settembre* near the Quirinal Palace, designed by Bernini and finished in 1670, is said to be the best of that great architect's churches, perfect in form and of gem-like beauty. In a chapel to the left of the high altar is the shrine of St. Stanislaus, and above the sacristy, the room where he died has been reconstructed.

The Carmelites

THE Feast of St. Teresa, together with the golden brown leaves of autumn, seem to cast a sort of Carmelite atmosphere around the mellow month of October. In Rome, October and April are the most beautiful months of the year; cool, brilliant in colour, with a luminous sky. St. Teresa, on her Feast, has it all her own way, for she also loved colour and sunlight.

The Carmelites have a number of convents and churches in Rome—that is only to be expected, for, as they say: "Where is Peter, there is Carmel".

A community of the Carmelite Friars of the Ancient Observance or "calced" (that is shod), is at the church of Our-Lady-Across-the-Bridge (*Santa Maria in Traspontina*). Pilgrims will pass it many times, for it is on the right of the wide thoroughfare that leads from the Tiber to St. Peter's.

An ancient church, it was rebuilt in the last century, and enshrines the body of St. Canute of Denmark, a great-nephew of the Canute who reigned in England. The Saint died in defence of the rights of the Holy See in 1086, and many miracles were worked at his tomb. One never knows what great Saint may lie buried in a Roman church; that is a characteristic of the Eternal City; its spiritual riches seem to be infinite.

The discalced Carmelites, or those of the Teresian Reform have their Generalate in a modern part of Rome: *Corso d'Italia,* next door to a fine large up-to-date parish church which they serve, called *Santa Teresa.*

Not far from there, in *Via Venti Settembre,* is another Carmelite church dedicated to Our Lady of Victory (not "victories" in the plural), because it was built in 1605 by Pope Paul V, in memory of the victory of Maximilian of Bavaria at Prague, when 25,000 Catholics routed four times

that number of Protestants. It is one of the most richly-
decorated of the smaller Roman churches. Its greatest
treasure, however, was the famous picture of Our Lady
of Victory carried by a Carmelite Friar at the Battle of
Prague. Destroyed by fire in 1620, it was replaced by
a good copy. Many visitors go to *Santa Maria della*

The Carmelite church dedicated to Our Lady of Victory

Vittoria to see the famous group of St. Teresa and the
Angel by Bernini, which is in the left transept. This group
has been much discussed, and the general opinion is that,
although good as a work of art, it is lacking in religious
feeling.

The church of Our Lady of the Stair (*Santa Maria della
Scala*) stands in the heart of the *Trastevere* (Across-the-
Tiber) region, near *Via della Lungara*. It enshrines a
miraculous picture of Our Lady which was originally
painted on the staircase of a neighbouring house. So

many answers to prayer were obtained on the spot, that the people of the region insisted on building a church dedicated to Our Lady and transferring the fresco to a place of honour over the high altar.

Next door is the Convent of the Discalced Carmelite Friars, who have charge of the church. They are proud of possessing an important relic of St. Teresa: nothing less than her foot. It is to be seen in a reliquary in a side chapel; it is small and must have been very graceful, and the famous incident in her life connected with that little foot comes vividly to mind. It happened in travelling, when a passerby noticed and admired her ankles; as a consequence of his flattering remarks, she introduced the coarse canvas stockings worn by her daughters to this day.

On the first floor of the Friary is the famous pharmacy of *La Scala,* over three hundred years old, redolent of the methods of ancient apothecaries. The Friars always used to turn out in great numbers during the terrible epidemics which devastated Rome in the past, and in consequence their healing art was venerated and trusted by the people of the *Trastevere* in those sad times, just as it is today.

The "pharmacy" is relatively small. On one side are windows looking into the cloister garth; the other sides are lined with glass-fronted cupboards of antique walnut. At the end, opposite the door, you will probably see a Friar at a small desk, busily writing prescriptions. Near the window, there will be another Friar intent on making pills with an ancient "pill-board". All the wood-work is very dark and handsomely carved in seventeenth century style.

In and above the cupboards are jars and boxes labelled with fascinating Latin names for extracts, elixirs and essences. Alembics and retorts stand on a shelf. One almost expects customers to come in asking for a "cure for a quartan ague" or "physick for the vapours".

Once, when the writer was present, a number of poorly dressed *Trasteverini* came in, knowing exactly what they wanted.   A labourer, in rags, asked for *Aqua della Scala;* this, it appears, is a special remedy for fevers of various kinds, and the Fathers alone possess the secret of its ingredients.   A poor woman with a baby wanted "elixir of paregoric", and a more stylish young lady asked for aspirin.   The Friars stock everything.

Their "Carmelite Cordial" is supposed to be made of herbs such as mallow, dandelion, bearsfoot, tansy and balm; but there again, one cannot penetrate the real secret of its manufacture.   In a small room opening out of the shop, there is a rare copy of an old "herbal", a large volume containing herbs and flowers carefully pressed, one to a page, with their properties minutely described on the opposite page.

Certainly, *Santa Maria della Scala* and her Friar apothecaries are off the beaten track frequented by tourists in a hurry; but if you have an hour or so to spare, you will be amply rewarded if you cross the *Ponte Sisto* (Pope Sixtus' Bridge) and make your way to Our Lady of the Stairs.   The entrance to the pharmacy is easy to recognise; and may you be lucky enough to see a Roman wine-cart which has driven in from Frascati or Marino, with its load of little barrels standing at the door, while the owner goes to get his breakfast and the horse munches his nosebag of hay.

The Franciscans

TO try to cover "Franciscan Rome" in the space of a brief chapter is like trying to put the famous ox in the well-known tea-cup. No more than a rapid survey can be attempted.

Let us begin in front of the Lateran Basilica—the Pope's Cathedral—where the beautiful bronze group of the Saint and his first companions stands as a worthy memorial to him. The Poor Little Man is seen in ecstasy, singing his Canticle of the Sun, while his companions, overcome with awe, stand or kneel, well-nigh in ecstasy also. This monument was raised in 1926 on the seven hundredth anniversary of St. Francis' death.

The spot on which it is placed is where Pope Innocent III met him when he, the Pope, was walking in the gardens that stretched from the Lateran to the Church of Holy Cross. History tells us that the Pontiff brushed him aside thinking he was just one more beggar, possibly with a sort of religious mania, for Francis had asked his approval for the founding of a new Order.

That night Innocent III saw in a vision the Church of Christ toppling to the ground, supported only by the ragged little man who had approached him in the gardens of the Lateran. Pontifical servants were sent early in the morning to scour Rome for the "beggar", and when at last he came into the Pope's presence he received not only leave to found his Order, but also the Pontiff's high approval and encouragement. And the Vicar of Christ was not too proud to beg pardon for having dismissed Francis in so summary a manner.

After his first visit Francis was a welcome and honoured guest in the Eternal City, though he never resided there for any length of time. However, sometimes he accepted the hospitality of a great and holy lady known as *Jacopa dei Sette Soli,* which might be translated "Jemima of the Seven Storeys".

Those "Seven Storeys" gave their name to her magnificent feudal castle, built on the ruins of the Imperial *Septizonium* erected on the Palatine by the Emperor

The bronze group of St. Francis and his companions looking towards the Lateran Basilica

Septimus Severus. It consisted of a seven-story edifice with columns, balconies and pilasters rising at the entrance to the Forum, to impress the stranger entering Rome. Later the Frangipani, Jacopa's family, fortified themselves in its remains. Jacopa had the privilege of being present at St. Francis' death, and when she in turn went to her eternal reward, was buried in the Lower Church at Assisi, close to the tomb of St. Francis. He was her guest in life in her

Roman stronghold, she was his guest in death, amid the cool shadows of the basilica.

To visit the Franciscan churches in Rome thoroughly would take about a fortnight, for there are no less than thirty-five of them. They range from the stately *Ara Coeli* on the Capitoline Hill, to new little churches in the remote suburbs.

The Ministers General of the three Franciscan "families", as they are called, reside in Rome. The Capuchin Generalate is in *Via Piemonte,* that of the Friars Minor in *Via Aurelia* on a spur of the Janiculum, and that of the Conventuals next door to the ancient church of the Holy Apostles, where the body of St. James is venerated.

Then the Franciscan "Cribs" at Christmas! That at the Holy Apostles is famous, so is the one at *Ara Coeli,* where the celebrated miraculous statue of the Holy Child is venerated. Then at St. Francis-on-the-River-Bank (*S. Francesco a Ripa*), in the *Trastevere,* is a small room where the Saint is said to have lodged and where an ancient portrait of him is shown.

On the Palatine, close to the site of Jacopa's fortress, is St. Bonaventure's church, where St. Leonard of Port Maurice is buried—he who originated the Stations of the Cross—and where outdoor Stations wind up a lonely pathway leading to his shrine.

At St. Anthony's near the Lateran, there is a vast modern church with an imposing International Franciscan College attached, where Friars from all parts of the world come to make their theological studies.

The Basilica of St. Sebastian, together with its catacomb, is under the care of Francicans, and so are St. Lawrence-Outside-the-Walls and the church on the Island in the Tiber where St. Bartholomew's relics are venerated. But we have mentioned only a few of the best known. Should any Tertians wish to visit them all, it would not be difficult to draw up the list.

The Franciscan connections with past Holy Years is

close indeed.   Thus, we learn that the Year of Jubilee in 1400, was proclaimed by Pope Boniface IX in Assisi itself.

In 1475 the Holy Year was proclaimed by a Franciscan Pope, Sixtus IV.   During the thirteenth Jubilee, in 1625, when Luke Wadding founded the Irish Franciscan house of St. Isidore's, a Third Order Princess in her habit, complete with a retinue of noble ladies also in their Third Order habits, arrived as pilgrims.   She was Princess Maria of Saxony.

Franciscan Tertiaries are warmly welcomed by the Pope, for he himself is a Franciscan Tertiary beside being a Dominican Tertiary as well.   To the Sovereign Pontiff alone belongs the privilege of this double membership.

The Passionists

AS the Passionist Fathers are so famous in England for their apostolic work, it is probable that many visitors to Rome will wish to see their churches, and perhaps, the Fathers themselves. At the Mother House they will find several English-speaking Fathers, and they will feel entirely at home. The Passionists have charge of two churches in the Eternal City.

First, there is the fine old church of SS. John and Paul on the Caelian Hill. It is of great antiquity, for its origin can be traced back to the time of Constantine. John and Paul were two brothers in the service of Constantia, daughter of the Emperor, who, during the persecution in the reign of Julian the Apostate, were beheaded and buried in their own dwelling.

At the end of the fourth century the powerful Christian Senator Pammachius, who numbered St. Jerome among his intimate friends, built a church over the house of the martyrs. This church was rebuilt and decorated by succeeding Popes, chief among them Adrian IV (Nicholas Breakspear), the only Englishman to be elected Pope. Thus the beautiful twelfth century colonnaded apse and the bell-tower are the work of the English Pontiff. The foundations of the tower formed part of the Temple of Claudius.

At the end of the eighteenth century the church was given to St. Paul of the Cross for the headquarters and Mother House of his newly-founded "Congregation of Barefooted Clerks of the Most Holy Cross and Passion of Our Lord Jesus Christ", generally known as "Passionists". Here the Founder lived and died, and his little chapel in a room in the bell-tower is still shown, as well as his cell, with its poor furniture.

His body lies in a sumptuous side chapel in the church itself; it is all of golden-coloured Sienese marble, lit by a golden stained-glass window, and ornamented with striking paintings of miraculous episodes in his life. Truly, the Congregation has erected a worthy memorial to its Founder.

The twelfth century bell-tower of SS. John and Paul, erected by the only English Pope

The neighbouring monastery is the residence of the Father General and his consultors, and here, young Passionists from all parts of the world come to complete their studies and training.

The church was the Titular Church of Cardinal Pacelli, before he was raised to the Chair of Peter. At present it is the Titular Church of Cardinal Spellman, Archbishop of New York. Recently interesting improvements have been made in the façade, which had been damaged by ill-chosen alterations wrought in the course of the centuries. The young Passionist Saint, Gabriel of the Seven Dolours is also buried in SS. John and Paul. Finally, one of the Fathers, a learned archaeologist, some years ago undertook excavations beneath the church, which led to the discovery of the Roman house belonging to the two martyrs. It is intensely significant with its well-preserved rooms, decorated with frescoes in the Pompeian style, and shows how rich Romans lived in the days of the Empire.

Church ceremonies are devotionally carried out at SS. John and Paul by the carefully-trained choir of Passionist students. It is quite easy to find, standing as it does, next to *San Gregorio,* whence St. Augustine set out to convert England.

The second Passionist stronghold is the *Scala Sancta,* or "Holy Staircase", with the church and monastery attached to it. It will be remembered that the first Passionist monastery in England was founded by the Ven. Father Dominic Barberi, in 1841, at Aston Hall in Staffordshire, and that Father Dominic received John Henry Newman into the Catholic Church. The Passionists were the first religious community in England to wear the habit in public, since the Reformation, and to observe a strict monastic life. Certainly the spirit of the Founder still hovers over the Mother House in Rome, and over the chapel where he lies in peace after a life devoted to prayer, penance and preaching.

The Column of the Scourging

THE Column of the Scourging of Our Lord stands in the old Church of St. Praxedes on the Esquiline Hill, close to St. Mary Major. It consists of half of the original pillar, the other half being still in Jerusalem. It is made of a kind of oriental jasper, and was brought to Rome about seven hundred years ago, by the famous Cardinal John Colonna, who was then Pontifical Legate in Palestine.

It is venerated with the greatest devotion by Romans and by pilgrims from all parts of the world, especially during the Lenten season, and shares with the relics at the Church of the Holy Cross and the *Scala Sancta,* or Holy Staircase, the popular devotion centring around the Passion of Our Lord.

The Church of St. Praxedes is dedicated to one of the daughters of a noble Roman, Cornelius Pudens the Younger, who was instructed in the faith by St. Peter himself, and who married the beautiful Claudia Rufina, daughter of the Welsh chief, Caractacus. The latter, with his family, was confined in Rome for about ten years after his defeat, and it is not surprising that his daughter married a Roman.

Originally built in the fourth century, the Church of *Santa Prassede,* as it is called in Italian, has been reconstructed several times, but the important relics which it enshrines have, happily, been left undisturbed. Among these relics are the bodies of the Saint herself and that of her sister, Saint Pudentiana, in ancient stone coffins, brought from the catacomb of Priscilla, in the ninth century.

It may be said, in passing, that the catacomb of Priscilla was constructed on the Salarian estate of the Lady Priscilla, their grandmother, that is, wife of Cornelius Pudens the Elder, Roman Senator and patrician. As both the young sister-Saints, Pudentiana and Praxedes, had the greatest veneration for the martyrs, tradition tells us that they used to collect the relics of the Christians who had died for their Faith, and when, owing to the violence of the persecution, they could not convey them to the outlying catacombs, for

Half of the original pillar at which Our Lord was scourged—a venerated relic in the church of St. Praxedes

the catacombs were all outside the city's limits, they reverently hid them in a well in their father's house. This well is still to be seen in the Church of St. Pudentiana.

Then, Pope Paschal I, in the ninth century brought the

J

body of St. Valentine from the catacomb named after him, and buried it near those of the two young Saints. Finally, before the end of his reign, this great Pope caused the relics of St. Zeno, and of over two thousand unnamed martyrs, to be transferred from the catacombs to this spot.

One might wonder why it was necessary to carry out transfers on such a large scale, but it should be remembered that at that period the Saracens were devastating the Mediterranean lands, and the Popes feared the desecration of the bodies of the martyrs, in case it should become impossible to defend the outlying Roman suburbs. They felt that there was a much greater chance of safety inside the walled city.

The Lenten Station is held at St. Praxedes on Monday in Holy Week. Much has been written about the "Stations" and, it is to be hoped, much more will be written in the future, for they are one of the oldest devotions in the Church, and form part of the tradition which links her indissolubly to apostolic times.

The "Stations" then, were in reality, visits made by the Pope, the clergy and the faithful of the city of Rome, in the earliest days of Christianity, or rather after the cessation of the persecutions, to the tombs of the martyrs in the different churches, there to watch and pray in preparation for conflict.

St. Gregory the Great, to whom England owes the Faith, arranged the ceremonial of the stational processions, appointed the churches to be visited, and the prayers to be recited. Thus the devotion is practised today as fixed thirteen centuries ago.

The series opens with the Station at Santa Sabina, the ancient Christian basilica which was presented by the Pope to St. Dominic and which the Friars Preachers have served ever since.

Spring comes early to Rome, and the almonds are beginning to flower in the neighbouring gardens, when, headed by the Cross the long procession passes out of the door of the church. It is composed of friars, priests, seminarians, men, women, and even children. As they sing the Litany of the Saints one comes to understand the Communion of Saints as never before. The evening shadows fall, blue and mysterious, and, to the chant of the *Vexilla Regis* the procession wends its way back for the final blessing with the relics, and the prescribed prayers. There is no Benediction of the Blessed Sacrament nor recitation of the Rosary; both of these devotions were instituted much later than the year 590, when the regulations for the Stations were laid down.

The Story of Saint Agnes

ON January 21st the Romans hold high festival in honour of their beloved little St. Agnes, and at the basilica where she is buried a Solemn High Mass is celebrated.

During Mass two lambs, symbols of St. Agnes' innocence, charmingly decked with flowers and bright ribbons are blessed by the officiating prelate. Afterwards they are blessed once more by the Holy Father himself. They are then placed under the care of the Benedictine nuns at St. Cecilia's. At Easter they are shorn, and their wool is woven into the *pallia* which are sent, as a sign of jurisdiction, to Archbishops and Patriarchs by the Pope in person.

St. Agnes is specially honoured today in two basilicas, that of St. Agnes-Outside-the-Walls, which stands above the catacomb of the same name where she was buried; and the Church of St. Agnes in the ancient Circus of Domitian, now called *Piazza Navona,* where the relic of her skull is reverently honoured.

Her parents' villa was situated on the wide *Via Nomentana,* and they placed their sumptuous gardens at the disposal of their fellow-Christians for the burial of the martyrs. There were many gardens of the same sort, as numbers of the early Christians were both rich and powerful. The persecutions did not always rage with the same violence; in fact they blazed up and died down with astonishing rapidity. Thus it came about that the Christians were not always hiding in the catacombs, and could go about at times with a certain measure of freedom, though never with a sense of complete security.

The villa on *Via Nomentana* was a popular meeting-place; friends arrived and departed constantly, there were even some aristocratic pagans who frequented it and who were rapidly falling under the spell of Christian ideals and teaching. They liked Agnes' family, and of course they all loved the beautiful little girl.

Some of this love was respectful and pure; but some was not. Agnes had coldly rejected the advances of the

The relic of St. Agnes's skull is venerated in her church in Piazza Navona built on the site of her martyrdom

son of the Prefect of the city, a young man of weak and ugly disposition. Her strength of character equalled her beauty of face and figure, and in the presence of that repulsive young man Agnes was like frozen steel.

He, on his side, did exactly what might have been expected. On the day following their final interview, Agnes happened to be sitting on a low marble bench in her favourite part of the garden. The folds of her white tunic and mantle fell in graceful lines to her little feet, shod in sandals of silvered doeskin.

Blossoming winter jasmine made a symphony of pale gold against the turquoise sky, and a fountain with a plume of white spray rose and fell among the green with a sound like music. She was alone in the villa except for the slaves —now freedmen— and her old nurse, Faustula.

Suddenly a tumult of voices shattered the silence. She rose, and crossing the garden quickly, turned the corner of the house to find herself face to face with a group of snarling guards, led by the Prefect's son. Faustula flung herself forward to save her beloved charge, but was pinioned by one of the legionaries.

Ethereal and lovely, Agnes silently held out her hands to be manacled. The leader had brought the smallest irons he had, but they slipped off her delicate wrists. The Prefect's son sprang forward to snatch her in his arms, but, at one glance from her steady eyes, he fell heavily to the ground, paralysed and blinded. At a nod from the captain, two guards stepped forward and bore him away in a matter-of-fact manner. His unpopularity was notorious.

At the Praetorium Agnes' calm statement of her faith, her steadfast refusal to offer incense to idols and her expression of love for Christ, almost moved the stony heart of the Praetor. But he turned to the Captain of the Guard and gave orders in a low voice. One of the soldiers overheard, glanced at Agnes and shuddered. The brutality of the order turned him sick.

Obeying to the letter, the guards led her to the Stadium of Domitian, a large oblong enclosure where games were held, surrounded by high tiers of seats. In the hollow space beneath the seats, the scum of the city ate, slept, quarrelled and sinned, living in horrible confusion.

It seemed truly as if all hell had been loosed against Agnes, God's white flower, now thrown mercilessly into that hotbed of nameless sins and obscenities. Never did her trust in her Lord waver, and never was trust more royally justified. She was miraculously protected by His divine power and totally unharmed.

The Captain of the Guard, baulked of revenge, ordered her to be consigned to the flames. But here also not a hair of her head was singed, not a flame touched her. Finally, the officer whose task it was to see that this beautiful Christian child should not live another day, ordered the strongest and most ferocious of his men to behead her, on pain of his own execution if he failed. And so, alone with her executioners, little Agnes gave up her pure soul to God.

And as the centuries passed devotion to the young Saint grew apace. Today we can pray beside her tomb, as the early Christians did, in the basilica by the catacomb, and we can venerate the holy relic of her head in her church in *Piazza Navona*.

Beneath the latter we can visit the excavated remains of the prison into which she was thrown between the various phases of her martyrdom. No wonder that her memory is kept alive by tender devotion, for her virtue has shone like a beacon through the ages. And no wonder that the Romans look upon her still as a beloved younger sister or cousin, and talk almost as if they were really related to her.

If you should go into one of the crowded streets in the poorer parts of the city and call out *"Agnese!"* (or the diminutive *"Agnesina!"*), heads will protrude from a score of windows and as many voices will shout *"Eccomi!"* ("Here I am!"). For, as I have already remarked, Agnes is greatly loved by the descendants of her fellow-citizens.

Saint Gregory's on the Caelian Hill

THAT St. Gregory's on the Caelian Hill should be the titular Church of His Eminence Cardinal Griffin places it at once in a position of double significance for English Catholics. Its original importance lies in the fact that it was the spot whence St. Augustine and his brother-monks set out to convert England, at the behest of Pope St. Gregory.

In the colonnaded court, beneath the shadows of the ancient arches, are several inscriptions that it is difficult to read unmoved. They are very plain and clear, without rhetoric or ornament. The first runs as follows: "From this monastery went forth: St. Gregory the Great, Founder and Father. St. Eleutherius, Abbot. Hilarion, Abbot. St. Augustine, Apostle of the English, first Archbishop of Canterbury. St. Lawrence, second Archbishop of Canterbury. St. Mellitus, Bishop of London. St. Justus, Bishop of Rochester. St. Paulinus, Bishop of York. Peter, third Archbishop of Canterbury."

Another inscription, of much less importance but deeply affecting, commemorates one Robert Peckham, an English gentleman, who was converted to the true Faith in the reign of Queen Elizabeth. On account of the persecutions, he could not live in England so he came to Rome; but in Rome he could not live because of his yearning for England, so he died. One of the few cases in history of a man dying of homesickness.

As the centuries went by other links with England were forged at San Gregorio. Both Cardinal Manning and Cardinal Vaughan were Titulars.

St. Gregory himself is one of the most majestic figures in the history of the Church. He was a member of the noble house of Anicia, being the son of Gordianus, a wealthy Roman Senator, and St. Sylvia. At his father's death he converted the family mansion on the Caelian Hill into a monastery of Benedictine monks. He himself entered the Order and held the office of Prior and Abbot, until he was raised to the Chair of Peter in 590.

When he dedicated the church and monastery, the dedication was to St. Andrew, but his successors changed it, and for that reason it is now known officially as "SS. Andrew and Gregory".

The church of St. Gregory on the Caelian Hill

The present entrance and atrium were built by another distinguished Titular, Cardinal Scipio Borghese in 1633, with the intention of embellishing the building, but completely changing the façade. The atrium and the interior of the church however, convey an impression of greater antiquity, in fact the walls and piers of the latter are said to be those of St. Gregory's time.

Opening off the right aisle is his monastic cell, with the stone slab on which he slept, and a marble episcopal chair which he is said to have used.

Near the left aisle in a chapel built by Cardinal Salviati, is a very ancient picture of Our Lady from which, according to tradition, the Saint heard the Mother of God speaking to him.

Beyond the church, near the cypress tree, seen in the background of our picture, are three ancient chapels built by St. Gregory. One of them, dedicated to St. Andrew, is most probably the original oratory in honour of that Saint. The second is dedicated to St. Sylvia, mother of St. Gregory, while the third, dedicated to St. Barbara, is also known as the "triclinium" or "dining-room of the poor". In it is a characteristic Roman table of marble with the typical carved "ball and claw" feet. It is said to be the original table at which St. Gregory daily served twelve poor men. The legend relates that one day a thirteenth guest appeared, who was an angel. After the meal the angel told St. Gregory that he was to succeed to the Chair of Peter.

The lovely legends which cluster round the life of the great Pope are depicted in various places in the church and the small chapels; but among the most interesting are those represented over the Saint's altar in St. Peter's, beneath which his holy relics lie in an ancient stone sarcophagus. A fine mosaic shows the Saint in the act of saying Mass, when, after the Consecration, bloodstains appeared on the corporal, to convert an unbelieving barbarian leader who happened to be present. The Holy Ghost, in the shape of a dove, is seen hovering close to St. Gregory's ear. And certainly the wisdom of his decisions, his writings and his words would easily encourage belief in continuous direct action of the Holy Spirit.

England has cause to be proud of her connection with a Pope of such great holiness and ability. A modern writer says of him: "He is a characteristically Roman figure—

virile, practical, with a great respect for law, and a high idea of what it can accomplish; but his concern for justice was no greater than his concern for charity. His last earthly deed was to send a warm winter cloak to a poor bishop who could not afford one.

"He was the first monk to be raised to the papal chair, but he proved himself an administrator of genius, and at the same time one of the greatest of Christian bishops, whose life and pastoral ideals were for centuries the inspiration and guide of the best among the Western clergy. His significance in the history of the papacy can hardly be overestimated."

The Church of St. Gregory is a touching reminder of this great Pope, and it is fitting that on his Feast the students of the English College in Rome should gather there to honour him who sent his missionaries to convert the northern Island. On the same day the students of the Beda College celebrate the Feast at his tomb, and it is good to hear the vault of St. Peter's echoing to the strains of "Faith of our Fathers".

Saint Lawrence in Rome

DURING his lifetime St. Lawrence, the young, holy and handsome deacon, almoner of the Pope and of rich Christians matrons who wished their goods to be distributed to the poor of Rome, was so beloved that his popularity has, it is said, never been equalled.

Perhaps Harry Hotspur and John Henry Newman each in his day, enjoyed parallel popularity, approaching St. Lawrence's but not equalling it. After his cruel martyrdom, and the sportsmanlike manner in which his holiness enabled him, like St. Thomas More, to jest with his executioners, there followed such a wave of conversions in Rome that a fresh persecution was launched against the Christians.

On August 10th, the Saint's skull is exposed for veneration in the Vatican. There is no doubt about its authenticity as it was found several centuries ago carefully guarded beneath the Pontifical altar in the Pope's private chapel in the Lateran Palace.

Together with the head of St. Lawrence (now in the Vatican), were discovered those of SS. Peter and Paul (now in the Lateran Basilica), and that of St. Agnes (now in the church built on the site of her martyrdom, in *Piazza Navona*).

St. Lawrence's head is entire and is kept in a jewelled reliquary of crystal and bronze, in which it is perfectly visible. It is an extraordinarily touching relic and seems still to bear the marks of the suffering which he underwent.

August 10th is traditionally the hottest day of the year in Rome, and as a rule the night sky is crossed by numbers of shooting stars, all in honour of *S. Lorenzo*.

The body of the martyr, together with that of St. Stephen, lies beneath the high altar in the ancient and strangely beautiful basilica of St. Lawrence-Outside-the-Walls. This basilica, being situated near one of the large railroad goods stations, was bombed on July 23rd, 1943, in an attempt to destroy a quantity of enemy war material. It is well known how the Holy Father hastened to the scene and wept undisguisedly as he knelt at the entrance, obstructed by fallen beams and rubble. The poor from the neighbouring slums surrounded him and wept with him.

The Basilica of St. Lawrence-Outside-the-Walls now restored after wartime bombing

A non-Catholic author and critic wrote as follows: "One of the most interesting of the major Roman churches, *San Lorenzo* has fortunately remained surprisingly unchanged since the Middle Ages. It stands on part of the ancient burial-ground in the *Campus Veranus,* of which the great cemetery of the *Campo Verano* close by is the modern descendant. The whole appearance of the church is one of great antiquity—the massive columns, the two beautiful ambones or pulpits, the Paschal candlestick, and the richly inlaid throne. The lovely canopy above the high altar is probably the earliest of the signed work of the Cosmati marble-workers who were active from the eleventh to the thirteenth century.''

On the Feast of St. Lawrence, a devout client of his might joyfully make a pilgrimage in his honour to many different parts of Rome. The itinerary would begin at the church of the *Navicella,* on the Caelian Hill, also known as *Santa Maria in Dominica,* where he was wont to distribute alms to the poor near the house of Ciriaca.

The "pilgrim way" would continue to *S. Lorenzo in Fonte,* a tiny oratory—one can hardly call it a church, it is so small—built on the spot in the slummy *Suburra* (still slummy today as it was during the Roman Empire), a valley between the Esquiline, the Quirinal and the Viminal Hills, where the Saint was thrown into prison, and where, like St. Peter, he converted his gaoler and caused a miraculous spring to flow so that the latter might be baptised. Hence "St. Lawrence of the Spring".

Then to *San Lorenzo in Panisperna,* on the site of his terrible martyrdom; it was better known to medieval Christians than it is to those of today. St. Gregory of Tours who visited Rome in the eleventh century speaks of it as one of the richest churches in the city.

Next the pilgrims will go to *San Lorenzo in Lucina,* St. Lawrence - on - the - Site - of - Lucina's - House, where the Christian matron Lucina, devoted to the memory of the Martyr, converted her house into an oratory in his honour. St. Lawrence's gridiron and his chains are venerated there. From the fourth century onwards it has played an important part in the history of the Church. Pontiffs were elected and Councils met within its walls.

Today very little of its antique architecture is visible excepting the porch and the belfry; it has been restored and embellished so many times that Pope St. Damasus, were he to return to the scene of his election (366), would not recognise it unless he were able, as he probably would be, to sense the undying spirit of devotion to St. Lawrence which inspired all the changes.

Finally, the "Laurentian" pilgrim should visit *San Lorenzo in Miranda* (Miranda's St. Lawrence), boldly and gloriously built right in the bosom of one of the finest pagan temples in the Roman Forum, dedicated to the deified Antoninus and his wife Faustina.   The effect is startling but glorious.   No special relic of the Martyr is kept there; it was built out of devotion to him in the fourteenth century by a well-to-do noble lady called Miranda. That is all we know of her; she is probably better pleased that the memory of her great Patron has survived while she herself is merely a name.

Santa Sabina

SANTA SABINA may truly be said to be the outward expression of the inner spirit of early Christianity. Its history is as long as it is interesting. Under the Roman Emperors, the Aventine Hill was an aristocratic quarter, where stood the house of the rich and handsome matron, Sabina, an aristocrat who was not ashamed to become the pupil of her Christian serving-maid, Seraphia. Once Sabina had embraced Christianity, martyrdom was not long in coming. She died by the sword in 114, and three centuries later, a well-known priest, Peter of Illyria, raised a noble church on the site of her house.

He constructed wisely and graciously. Fastidious about his materials, he took a whole series of fine Corinthian columns from the neighbouring Temple of Diana. He set them well apart and surmounted them with a series of arches. The whole building has been described as "Hellenic in its clean austerity". The polychrome design in coloured marble above the arches, and in the pavement, is characteristic of the best fifth century decoration. Succeeding Pontiffs embellished *Santa Sabina*. The entrance was guarded by two magnificent doors of carved wood, dating from the fifth century. It seems almost miraculous that such a work of art should have survived for fifteen hundred years, in spite of dangers from fire, earthquake and barbarian invasions. Only ten panels out of twenty-eight have disappeared in the course of the ages.

The top right-hand panel, showing with primitive simplicity the Crucifixion of Our Lord between two thieves, is the earliest known representation of the Crucifixion; other artists showed the Cross in their mosaics, but always the Cross without a figure, jewelled and ornamented. Crucifixion being the death of a slave, Christians were still too near the central event of the redemption to show it otherwise than as a triumph; hence they avoided the more realistic rendering to which we are accustomed today.

However, the anonymous woodcarver at *Santa Sabina* probably wished to convey in all its stark reality what Our Lord's death on the Cross meant to him. At least three

Columns from the Temple of Diana were used in the building of the fifth century church of Santa Sabina

hundred years more were to elapse before painters and sculptors found the courage to follow his example.

In the course of the tenth century, the Aventine Hill began to bristle with fortresses and towers, notably the stronghold built by the Savelli, where two future Popes (Honorius III and Honorius IV) were born.

K

When Honorius III wished to bestow a suitable church and convent on St. Dominic in 1220, he could think of nothing better than to give him the church with a large piece of adjoining land, which belonged to his family domain and stood next to their castle. Thereon was built a stately Friary, its beautiful cloister bearing witness to the genius of the architects who worked for St. Dominic and his sons. The cell which the Saint occupied is still to be seen, small and simple almost like a prison cell, with white-washed walls and a window looking into the church.

In front of the high altar in the church is a simple slab of marble bearing the words: "On this stone, the holy Father, St. Dominic spent nights prostrate in prayer". Not far from it is a smooth, black stone, about the size and weight of two large flatirons joined; the legend relates that the devil hurled it at St. Dominic in an effort to interrupt his converse with God. But hard-headed scholars say that it was an ancient Roman weight from a neighbouring market. They are probably right.

In the middle ages the Station ceremonies at *Santa Sabina* were more elaborate than they are today. Both the clergy and the people, in greater numbers than for the subsequent Lenten Stations, used to meet in the morning at the Church of St. Anastasia, at the foot of the Palatine Hill, to await the coming of the Pope. In his presence, a Cardinal blessed the ashes and distributed them to all present, including the Pope. All received the ashes barefoot and with great respect. A procession was then formed, followed by the Pope, also barefoot, chanting the Litany of the Saints as it ascended the hill to *Santa Sabina,* where Mass was solemnly celebrated.

Certainly today, larger numbers of the faithful gather at *Santa Sabina* than at any other Station. All the Dominicans from the Roman Convents and Colleges meet there, and the sight of their white habits and black cloaks in that austere church, splashed with early spring sunshine, is unforgettable.

Saint Clement's

YOU *must not* miss St. Clement's Basilica, though it is not mentioned in any of the "great tours" of Rome. "Peter, Linus, Cletus, Clement," so runs the majestic list of the early Popes. Clement was a rich and powerful Roman patrician, a personal friend and convert of St. Peter's, who placed his spacious house at the disposal of the Apostle for meetings with his neophytes. As Bishop of Rome, Clement wrote a famous letter of direction and admonition to the Church of Corinth, while St. John was still alive. He is traditionally identified with the Clement who was the fellow-labourer St. Paul mentioned in the Epistle to the Philippians.

According to the ancient legend, St. Clement was sent into exile under Trajan and was thrown into the Black Sea with an anchor tied to his neck. The legend goes on to tell how every year on the Feast of the Saint (November 23rd) the waters used to recede from the place of his martyrdom, showing a marble shrine containing his body. In fact there is an antique fresco in the lower basilica relating how a child left behind at the shrine on one such occasion, was recovered safe and sound the following year. The relics of the Saint, for long venerated in the Crimea (in spite of the legendary underwater shrine) were brought to Rome in the year 868 by the brothers SS. Cyril and Methodius, Apostles of the Slav people, and deposited in St. Clement's Basilica by Pope Adrian II.

There are at present three buildings, one superimposed upon the other, and all three may be visited. The lowest probably formed the ground floor of a great palace belonging to Clement's family, and it has been suggested that the Popes lived in it until the Emperor Constantine gave them the Lateran. Certainly there was an Oratory of St. Clement on the spot before the end of the persecutions.

When you go down there you can hear the mysterious sound of waters flowing day and night.   They are the

St. Clement's Basilica as it is today

"hidden waters of Rome" probably coming from some broken and long-forgotten aqueduct in the neighbourhood. When the Dominican Fathers, who own the property, began to excavate, streams of water rushed in and formed a lake beneath the basilica.

It was owing to the generosity of the late Cardinal O'Connell, Titular of St. Clement's from 1911 to 1944, that a tunnel 40 feet below the ground level was bored for a distance of 700 yards to connect the excavations with the *Cloaca Maxima* or great drain (built by the Etruscans) and to allow the hidden waters to reach the Tiber. Thus St. Clement's was saved from destruction.

The second building (now known as the subterranean basilica) was built on top of the lowest one, shortly after the Edict of Milan (313) by which Christians were allowed to practise their religion openly. It seems that it was formed out of the upper floor of the palace or "house of Clement". There are many interesting frescoes in it, some of which are over a thousand years old.

However, to summarise a long and thrilling history, in course of time this "subterranean basilica" was abandoned, and after 1084 when the Normans wrecked it, as well as the neighbouring buildings, what remained was filled in with rubble and upon its walls and pillars the present-day magnificent basilica was built. It was finished before 1099, because we know that Pope Paschal II was elected in the Conclave held there, in that year. When the underground basilica was brought to light (between 1857 and 1868) 130 cart loads of rubble were removed from it.

The church and property were bestowed upon the Irish Dominicans by the Stuarts during the Cromwellian persecutions in Ireland.

The upper basilica is perfect in form and proportion, and corresponds exactly with the shape of the ancient Imperial basilicas. The beautiful Cosmatesque pavement recalls the brilliance of a Persian carpet, wrought in semi-precious marbles and stone. The pillars are all much older than the church itself, and were probably taken from the Roman Forum: some are of smooth Oriental granite, some of Parian marble, fluted; and some of polished Numidian marble.

In the centre is seen the beautifully ornamented choir with its twin pulpits. Underneath the ancient altar are the relics of St. Clement, Pope and Martyr, of St. Flavius Clemens, Consul and Martyr, and of St. Ignatius of Antioch, Martyr, who is believed to have been one of the children whom Our Lord gathered in His arms, when He said "suffer little children to come unto Me".

In the apse is the most beautiful of all medieval mosaics, the symbolic representation of the Triumph of the Cross.

One of the frescoes in the lower basilica, dating from about 1000, is important and specially interesting. It shows St. Clement in Gothic vestments, wearing the pallium, and celebrating Mass at an altar upon which are the altar-cloth, the missal, chalice and paten. He is pronouncing the words *Dominus Vobiscum* with hands extended as in the Mass today.

The upper part of the fresco, cut by the floor of the upper basilica, shows him being enthroned by his predecessors, SS. Peter, Linus and Cletus.

Among the congregation depicted at St. Clement's Mass is one Sisinius who came to mock and not to pray, but was struck blind in consequence; on the right of the picture a servant is seen leading him away. Nevertheless, in the lower part of the fresco, although his sight has been restored by the Saint, he returns to arrest St. Clement as a magician, and orders his servants to drag the Saint off to prison. But the servants are only removing a large pillar (which they imagine to be St. Clement) while Sisinius stands by giving directions, also under the same illusion.

We have merely touched the surface of some of the wonderful things in St. Clement's. Don't miss it if you can possibly help it. Its significance is inestimable.

St. John at the Latin Gate

SOME lovers of Rome hold that the ancient Church of St. John at the Latin Gate is the most romantic of all the city's churches. There is a good deal to be said for this opinion. The *Via Latina*, or Latin Way, one of the great Roman roads, led southwards to Capua, and still preserves something of the mystery of the middle ages, if not of Imperial Rome.

Dedicated to St. John the Evangelist, the church was built in the fifth century and although much of what we see today belongs to a later period, yet a great part of its interior and noble arcaded vestibule belong to the original building.

Placed where it is, it particularly commemorates what is called St. John's "martyrdom" when he was plunged in a cauldron of boiling oil, and miraculously emerged unhurt. It stands in a solitary spot, shaded by a towering cedar, near which is an ancient Byzantine well-head.

The interior is ornamented by frescoes depicting scenes from Bible history. The whole impression conveyed by both exterior and interior is one of aloof and ancient beauty translated into brick and stone. It has about it something of the spirit of the "beloved disciple"; just how it is hard to say; such things cannot really be put into words, and still less can the spirit of St. John's love for his Master be expressed in language. We know, of course, that he was originally a disciple of St. John the Baptist, that he was the son of Zebedee and Salome, and brother to St. James the Greater, that he was engaged in fishing with his father and brother when he was called by Christ, and that he had the sublime experience of resting his head close to the Sacred Heart during the Last Supper.

We know also, of course, that he alone of the Apostles remained faithful to the Master during His Passion, and that to him Christ entrusted the care of His Blessed Mother. After the Ascension and the descent of the Holy Ghost, with Peter he was prominent in organising the Church. He went later to Asia Minor and thence was recalled to Rome on account of a new persecution which had broken out

The ancient church of St. John at the Latin Gate

under Domitian. There he was condemned to be cast into a cauldron of boiling oil, near the Latin Gate, and as already stated, he emerged from the terrible ordeal unscathed.

The beautiful little octagonal chapel which stands close to the church marks what is held to be the exact spot where the cauldron was placed.   It is called *San Giovanni in Olio* ("St. John of the Oil"), and was built by one Benedict Adam, a French prelate, who was an Auditor (i.e., a Judge) of the Tribunal of the Rota in 1508.   It was designed by a follower of the great Bramante and though small it is in perfect proportion and taste.   It replaced a small medieval chapel which stood on the same spot.

By a happy arrangement all is now under the care of the Fathers of Charity, who have cleaned and restored the church and the adjoining buildings.   They now form the residence of the Father General of the Institute and a house of studies for the younger members.   These Fathers, sometimes known as "Rosminians", especially in England, live a life of true charity in its widest sense, beginning with the love of God; "one thing is necessary . . . "   The essential state of the members is that of close union with God through prayer and the practice of virtue.   And, they hold, since the love of God implies the love of man, they should be ready to undertake all works of charity of every kind, whether spiritual, intellectual or corporal.   What better place could they have found for their Mother House than the spot sacred to the Apostle who spent his last days saying: "Little children, love one another"?

The Catacombs

THE catacombs you *must* visit. They are on the Appian
Way, the famous road along which St. Paul came from
Pozzuoli to Rome. It runs from the Eternal City to
Brindisi, was built in the year 312 B.C. and is probably
the most celebrated of all the Roman roads in the world.

A great part of it is still unspoiled, and to walk along
it, beneath the ancient pines, with the remains of Roman
tombs on either side, and the mauve and pink of the Alban
Hills faint on the horizon, is to live once more in the
Apostolic times. A famous French writer, Abbé Henri
Perreyve says: "Look and listen; listen to the silence of
Rome among the ruins on the Appian Way; and that
listening will fill your soul for the rest of your life." So if
possible either walk or drive as far as you can along it.

"Catacombs" as such, are situated on most of the roads
leading out of the city. There are fourteen principal ones;
their galleries if placed end to end would stretch for a
distance of some 700 miles.

All Catholics have a vague idea of the catacombs, but
those who visit them for the first time will be surprised at
the unexpected wonders revealed in them. That is why
it will be well if each pilgrim goes armed with a pocket
flashlight. Electricity is not always available for lighting
the long galleries. Although the authorities provide a small
candle for each visitor, yet there are often inscriptions or
details of the martyrs memorials that one would wish to
see much more clearly.

Secondly, should you be here during the summer months
when the Roman heat is at its height, do not, above all,
forget to take a coat when you go to the catacombs. This
sounds ridiculous, but only those who have experienced it,
can describe the deadly chill that strikes to the very bones
when one enters those underground passages, after leaving

the outside world rejoicing in a temperature of 90 degrees. The reason is easy to understand; and no one could possibly wish for air-conditioning to be introduced into those sacred places. It would be almost like putting a lift in them.

The catacombs were originally the burial places of the Christians, and were known to them as *coemeteria* or

The "Crypt of the Popes" in the Catacomb of St. Callistus

"resting places", in reference to the Resurrection. Long galleries or tunnels were hollowed out of the soft Roman rock, and along the sides were cut niches for the bodies of the Christians. During periods of active persecution they were used as places of refuge, so it came about that, as time went on, innumerable secret exits were provided, as well as traps for the pursuers, such as stairs that ended in a deep pit and corridors that led nowhere. In some places, cunningly-masked openings still give access to quarries through whose crumbling galleries the refugees might safely reach the upper air.

The more important Roman families or groups, sometimes owned large recesses resembling small low-roofed mortuary chapels, hollowed out in the rock at right angles to the galleries, and ornamented with stucco and paintings. Many of them were sacred to the martyrs, and the stone coffin enclosing the martyr's body was so arranged that Mass might be celebrated upon it. This was the origin of the custom of enclosing relics of the martyrs in the altar-stone in Catholic churches.

One of the most interesting of these chapels is "the crypt of the Popes" in the catacomb of St. Callistus, which is conveniently and quickly reached by bus from the Colosseum. A number of the early Popes are buried in it, as shown by the inscriptions on the walls. It contains an altar, and Mass is celebrated there daily.

To hear Mass in the catacombs is an inestimable privilege, fraught with devotion, and with the realisation of our utter "oneness" with the Church through the centuries; the Apostolic age becomes a real and tangible thing; we pray and offer the divine Sacrifice in union with the first Christians, the glorious forerunners of our own times; times in which persecutions are again proving that "the blood of the martyrs is the seed of the Church".

The Mamertine Prison

THE Mamertine Prison, situated at the foot of the Capitoline Hill, close to the Roman Forum, is a terrible place, in which SS. Peter and Paul were held in captivity for eight or nine months. Their survival after such an experience seems in itself a miracle.

The prison is a very ancient one, said to have been built by Servius Tullius, one of the Kings of Rome, about the year 600 B.C. Hence its historical name, the *Tullianum*.

It consists of two circular cells hewn out of the solid rock, one below the other. There is a circular opening in the ceiling of the lower one through which enters light and air—that is to say, practically none of either—and through which prisoners were let down by means of a rope. There is a staircase today, of course, to allow the faithful to venerate this hallowed spot. We are told that when the Numidian rebel Jugurtha in 104 B.C. was lowered into it, pending his execution, he exclaimed: "What cold baths you Romans have!" It was, in fact, generally used as a prison for specially dangerous characters, considered to be enemies of the State, and for criminals condemned to death. Existence in the lower chamber was particularly painful when the upper one was full, for then absolutely no light nor air came into it.

In the year 66 SS. Peter and Paul were cast into this awful place, by order of Nero. Reflecting on Nero's atrocities, one realises how true are the words of scripture: "Vengeance is mine, saith the Lord". At the extreme end of *Via Nomentana,* there is to be seen the spot where Nero, a coward, flying from his pursuers, entered a slave's hut and there fell upon his sword, dying a miserable, lonely death, hated by all.

We can imagine the Apostles in the Mamertine surrounded by thick darkness, and in an atmosphere which was almost unbreathable. The prison was so intensely damp and cold that confinement in it was worse than death. The Roman historian Sallust, describes it as "a dark, filthy, frightful den, twelve feet underground, walled in, and covered with massive stones".

In the Mamertine Prison

But nothing could daunt Peter and Paul. We read in the lessons of the Roman Breviary for July 2nd, that, while in this dreadful dungeon, they converted Processus and Martinian, captains of their guard, together with forty-seven fellow prisoners.

It is well, while standing there to imagine fifty-one people herded in the narrow space; that is, the two Saints, the two captains and the forty-seven others. It must have been something like the Black Hole of Calcutta. As there was no water with which to baptise the neophytes, St. Peter caused a miraculous spring to come forth from the rock. The little spring is there to this day, marked by a circle of stone.

The description given of the Mamertine by Charles Dickens after he had visited it, is more wordy than that of Sallust, but the ideas are much the same. He was evidently impressed, for he says: "The thing lives as a distinct and separate memory in my thoughts. It is very small and low-roofed, silent, close and tomblike; the dungeon is so black and stealthy (did he mean 'filthy'?) and stagnant and naked that this dark spot is a nightmare within a dream."

The Apostles were chained to the low column seen in the photograph.

On the walls of the vestibule of the upper prison, are inscriptions giving lists of all those imprisoned there in succeeding years. Among them are St. Hippolytus, St. Paulina, St. Eusebius and St. Marcellus.

Regarding St. Marcellus, we may recall that, although Pope and successor of the Prince of the Apostles, he was sent to work in the Emperor's stables where the fleetest horses were kept for the Imperial post. This heavy work soon broke his constitution, yet before he died he was taken to the Mamertine Prison. After his death, his holy body was buried in the catacomb of St. Priscilla, and the stables where he had laboured were turned into an oratory by the Christians, in the reign of Constantine. Four centuries later his relics were taken from the catacomb and placed beneath the high altar of the fine church built on the site of the oratory.

The Colosseum

ONE of the finest places to visit alone, without a guide, is the Colosseum, provided one is armed with some information beforehand. As a ruin, it is unique in the world, being a great amphitheatre, oblong in shape and three storeys high. Inside, surrounding the vast arena, were tiers of seats (the supports of which may still be seen) capable of accommodating eighty-five thousand people. The description of the interior given by Cardinal Wiseman in *Fabiola* is well worth reading. Enough of it is still preserved to give a clear idea of what it must have been in the days of the Roman Empire. It was begun by the Emperor Vespasian in the year 70, and finished by Titus ten years later. Architecturally it is a magnificent structure with the interesting peculiarity of showing, in the half-columns of the exterior, the three "orders", Doric, Ionic and Corinthian. The whole building was originally coated with marble and the many holes in the walls were made by barbarians wrenching away the bronze clamps which held the slabs of marble in position.

Inside, the arena was always kept covered with clean sand, and in summer a light silken awning was spread across it by the sailors of the Imperial fleet. It seems incredible that an awning of such size should have been available, nevertheless the fastenings which held it are still visible in the uppermost portions of the outer wall.

It will be well worth while to make the ascent to the highest parts of this extraordinary edifice. The entrance to the stairs is through a gate under the colonnade on your right as you leave the arena.

From the upper galleries one realises the magnitude of this vast amphitheatre and what an opportunity it provided for spectacular exhibitions, involving as they did, the lives of thousands of slaves, gladiators and Christian martyrs.

By the time that Christianity was spreading, the Christians were eagerly seized upon as a possible innovation in the cruel combats known as "games". It would be a much better sight, thought the pagans, to see Christians thrown to the wild animals than to have mere hired pugilists or gladiators struggling against each other.

St. Ignatius of Antioch, Bishop of that city, was sent to

The Colosseum floodlit by night

Rome in the year 107 to be killed by wild beasts in the arena. His holy remains were buried in the neighbouring church of St. Clement's, where they are still venerated. The last Christian to die there was St. Telemachus, an Eastern monk, who threw himself into the arena in an endeavour to stop the gladiatorial combats, and was stoned to death by the infuriated mob cheated of its sanguinary amusement.   It is said that, in consequence, the Emperor Honorius suppressed gladiatorial shows forever.

From earliest times the Colosseum has been the centre of reverent pilgrimages.   A significant story is told of Pope St. Gregory the Great.   The ambassadors of the Eastern Emperor Mauritius, being in Rome, asked him for some relics of the martyrs to take back with them to be honoured in the churches of Constantinople.   St. Gregory bade one of his suite accompany them to the Colosseum and give them a handful of sand gathered from the arena itself.   Highly indignant, the Eastern diplomats returned to the Pope and said that such a gift was an insult to them as well as to their Imperial master.   St. Gregory made no reply, but silently took the cloth containing the sand and squeezed it gently.   The astounded officials saw drops of blood trickle from it.   Our own Venerable Bede, in the eighth century made the famous prophecy: "While the Colosseum stands, Rome will stand; when the Colosseum falls, Rome will fall; when Rome falls, the world will fall."

The Island in the Tiber

A^T the expense of the Commune of Rome, the Island in the Tiber has been illuminated and decorated in honour of a Saint who died four hundred years ago.

St. John of God was born in Portugal in 1495. First he tended sheep, then he enlisted as a soldier in the Portuguese army, and finally, overcome with pity for the Christian slaves captured by the Moors, he disguised himself as a pedlar and thus brought them help and consolation. Making his way to Spain and realising something of the terrible conditions of the sick in the public hospitals of his day, he settled in Granada to tend the suffering and the dying and laid the foundation of his Order known as the "Hospitallers of St. John of God".

That was in 1540. He died in 1550; and his Order still flourishes in several countries. He was canonised in 1690 and later, together with St. Camillus of Lellis, was named patron of hospitals, of nurses and of the sick.

The Hospital of St. John's Order was established on the Island in the Tiber by no less a person than Pope St. Pius V, the saintly Dominican Friar who instituted the Feast of the Most Holy Rosary. We are told that in the great triumphal entrance of Don Juan of Austria into Rome after the victory of Lepanto in 1571, the conqueror was accompanied by a poor religious in a black dress. This was Sebastian Arias of the Brothers of St. John of God. It was on Don Juan's recommendation that the Pope approved the Order and gave the Brothers a monastery and hospital on the island.

Shaped like a ship, the small island stems the rapid current of the Tiber and seems to float peacefully on its waters.

The ancient historians relate that in the year 509 B.C., in the height of summer, a few months after the infamous

King Tarquin and his followers had been driven by the
infuriated populace to seek refuge in exile, the broad corn-
fields between the hills and the Tiber were a sea of rippled
gold.   But the pagan priests told the people that corn
planted and grown under the sway of a tyrant was accursed
and unfit to make bread for honest men.

The Hospital of the Brothers of St. John of God on the boat-shaped
Island in the Tiber

Armed with knife and sickle they cut down the rich
harvest and flung it into the river.   The tangled mass of
stalks and ears of corn stranded on a sandbank and in
time it solidified, forming the island.

With the growth of Rome's power and magnificence, the
island was transformed into the likeness of a huge marble
ship with an obelisk for mast. In 292 B.C. it was dedicated
to Aesculapius, the god of healing, as a temple.   Sick

slaves were left in the temple precincts and if they were cured were given their freedom; if they died, well, there was the Tiber into which they might conveniently be thrown. From that time to the present day, the care of the sick has formed the principal work of those who live on the island.

About the year A.D. 983, the Emperor Otho III built a church on the site of the ancient temple, to receive the body of the Apostle St. Bartholomew which had been brought from Lipari to Benevento in 809, and from Benevento to Rome in 983, where it has remained. Hence the Island is known as the Isle of St. Bartholomew.

It was in a hospital there, that in the reign of King Henry II one of the officers of his court, a certain Rahere who had come to Rome as a pilgrim, was nursed back to health after a serious illness. When he returned to London, out of gratitude to the Apostle whose relics he had venerated on the island, he put aside a portion of his great fortune for the foundation of St. Bartholomew's Hospital. Thus closely is "Bart's" linked to the Eternal City, thanks to Rahere's devotion to the Saint.

Opposite the larger church with its ancient bell-tower, is a smaller one, incorporated in the hospital; it is dedicated to St. John Calybites (from *"calube"* or "hut"), a recluse of the fifth century whose life resembles that of St. Alexius. The son of a rich nobleman, he secretly left his home to become a monk. Returning after six years disguised as a beggar he dwelt in a poor hut near his father's house and only revealed his identity to his mother as he lay dying. His relics are still kept in the church which has given its name to the hospital.

However, among the Romans, the hospital is always called of the *"Fatebenefratelli"* which means "the Brothers-Who-Do-Good". "Do Good" was the constant saying of the Founder to his Brothers, and the phrase is forever connected with them. About twenty years ago the ancient hospital buildings were repaired and completely modernised, so that today it is one of the best hospitals in the city, with a variety of departments under the direction of eminent practitioners; in fact it is second to none in general medicine, surgery, eye-ear-and-throat departments, a child-welfare clinic, a complete X-ray installation and special departments for skin diseases and dental surgery.

St. Michael's Roman Fortress

THERE are many aspects of *Castel Sant' Angelo,* St. Michael's Castle, the subject being well-nigh inexhaustible. During the reign of St. Gregory the Great, in 590, a terrible plague affected Rome. In order to free the city from the scourge a vast procession, or rather series of processions, made their way through the streets, praying to Our Lady "Salvation of the Roman People". As they passed along the banks of the Tiber a vision of St. Michael sheathing his sword was seen above the huge circular tomb of the Emperor Hadrian; it was the highest point in the neighbourhood, and the vision meant that God would no longer punish the people. Then the plague ceased. Since that time there has always been a statue of St. Michael sheathing his sword, on the summit of the fortress.

The castle may be considered from the historical point of view, or the architectural, or the artistic, or the military, for it was one of the most important strongholds in Italy, and held the line of the Tiber, just as Oxford used to hold the line of the Thames, and Stirling that of the Forth. Originally built by the Emperor Hadrian as a tomb for the Imperial family, it was fortified during the succeeding centuries, decorated by the Popes who resided there in the sixteenth century, and today it contains, besides many art treasures, a most interesting arsenal of medieval arms, armour and engines of war.

In the upper courtyard of the Castle stone balls, for use in powerful catapults, were stacked. Each pile was placed in front of a marble slab let into the wall, with an inscription stating exactly the number of the balls in the pile, and the weight of each. In the centre is an ancient statue of St. Michael, not sheathing his sword, but with it raised, as it were in salute or in defence.

The first door on the right, in front of which are some rough fragments of stone, leads to a delightfully authentic reconstruction of a room in the guard-house, where the officer and men on duty would have spent much of their time.   There are the antique beams of the ceiling; the old rough walls; a fireplace with its chimney-hood decorated

"St. Michael's Cat" suns himself on one of the largest catapults

with the papal arms; a dresser with medieval earthenware plates and dishes; a copper kettle, a spit and a skillet hanging near the fire; breastplates, helmets and pikes ranged against the wall; an old oak refectory table, with a smaller table for the Captain of the Guard, bearing his leather-bound log-book, goose-quill pen, inkhorn and pounce-box, all ready to hand.

Some early muskets, such as were used when gun-powder was first invented, hang on the walls, along with a brass bugle and an iron lantern.

In another courtyard is a wonderful collection of catapults and arbalests, complete down to the last detail with cords, bolts, locks and triggers.   One of the largest catapults is seen in our illustration, with St. Michael's cat sunning himself luxuriously beneath the steel-braced socket with its heavy stone missile.   Surely even an Archangel can have a cat in his fortress, to defend the larder against invading mice, if nothing else.

A non-Catholic writer says it is the oldest still-inhabited castle in the world, and by far the most romantic in history—being a tomb, a prison, a fortress and a palace. The fortified wall which connects it with St. Peter's and the Vatican contains a corridor along which the Popes might pass to take refuge from threatened attack on the Vatican.

The worst siege and sack of Rome took place in 1527, when Lutheran troops led by the Constable of Bourbon put it to fire and sword.   Clement VII was saved by flight along this passage, after the Swiss Guard had died to a man, in defence of his person.   A faithful attendant who accompanied him threw his own mantle over the Pontiff so that he should not be recognised as he passed the loopholes in the covered corridor, in the wall.   He was thus saved, while Rome underwent the worst period of plunder and desecration that it had ever known.

A small chapel used to stand on the summit of the Castle, dedicated to "St. Michael in the Clouds", and many devout clients of the Archangel used to gather there. Today also we gather around him.   For what better protection can humanity have, in the presence of atheistic materialism, than St. Michael who leads men against the forces of evil, with his stupendous battle-cry: "Who is like unto God?"

The Forum

THERE is a tendency to say: "Oh, yes, the Forum, that's ancient pagan Rome; but *I* am interested in Christianity". Certainly; but there is a great deal more in the Forum directly connected with Christianity than you would think. Don't miss it if you can possibly find time for a visit.

Our photograph shows the corner of an ancient temple of Saturn with the dome of a church dominating the background. It is a beautiful symbol of the manner in which the ways of Providence have worked. What is left of the pagan temple is stately and beautiful; but its essence, its significance, has crumbled. It means nothing more than fragmentary architectural beauty.

Whereas, the church which appears behind it is dedicated to St. Luke and St. Martina, and is built over the library of the Roman Senate, where the records of great military and political achievements were stored. Nothing is left of them today, and upon the site stands the church. St. Luke, whose pen recorded the greatest events the world has ever known is honoured there, together with the young martyr, Martina, who died in torment, after converting her gaoler.

An Evangelist and a Martyr are indeed appropriate as patrons of such a place of worship. And, as the sun sets behind the dome, which recalls in a certain way that of St. Peter's, one can almost read in the golden vision of the clouds, the well-known words: "God is glorified in all His saints".

Then, when you have crossed the centre of the Forum, a wide space littered with the ruins of shops, temples and triumphal arches, you will come to the famous *Basilica Julia,* a vast building erected by Julius Caesar for the transaction of public business. Only its outline, the bases of the five rows of columns, and the portico are still discernible; but they take on a new meaning when we understand that they provided the exact ground plan and arrangement of aisles and pillars for the glorious basilica erected on the Ostian Way, over the tomb of the Apostle Paul, known throughout the centuries as St. Paul's-Outside-the Walls. There are much better things to come when you have gone on beyond the *Basilica Julia*. You enter a kind of wonderland of immense walls, roofed over,

The crumbling remains of the Temple of Saturn overshadowed by the dome of a church dedicated to an Evangelist and a Martyr

and presenting all the characteristics of a Christian church though in a partially ruined condition. You look more carefully and you see that the walls were once elaborately frescoed and that large portions of the frescoes remain.

You see numbers of saints painted with that devotional simplicity which characterises all art of the period. It certainly was a remote period, for, while Christian artists were working there, good King Alfred was ruling

England, and Charlemagne was the Emperor of the West.

One of the most striking and best-preserved of these frescoes shows Our Lord seated on an Imperial throne, with the Saints and Fathers of the Eastern Church on one side, and those of the West on the other. The close union of East and West is thus graphically shown, especially as these paintings were executed before certain parts of the East broke away from allegiance to the Sovereign Pontiff.

The building was used originally as a place of worship in the fourth or fifth century, situated as it was, right in the heart of the palace of the Emperor Augustus. It was dedicated to Our Lady. So, as the years went by, it came to be known as *Santa Maria Antiqua* ("St. Mary's the Old"). In one of the side aisles, in a small niche, there is a little fresco which is unique in the world and which is happily in a good state of repair.

In it are seen the figures of three women represented with haloes, each of them holding a child in her arms. After a brief reflection one sees that the artist has given in one picture: Our Blessed Lady holding her Divine Child; her own mother St. Anne holding her when she was an infant; and St. Elizabeth holding St. John the Baptist. Would that a reproduction were possible. But the position of the niche is awkward and the light very bad.

On leaving, we pass a large decorated oratory of the same period, dedicated to the Forty Martyrs of Sebaste, who were deeply venerated by the early Christians.

At the opposite end of the Forum stands a fine church with a soaring bell-tower of tawny-red brick. It was built in the eleventh century and is called *Santa Maria Nuova* ("Our Lady the New"), because the increasingly ruinous condition of "Our Lady the Old" made it necessary to abandon it. Thus, another lovely church to honour Our Blessed Mother, and to stamp out the remaining vestiges of dying paganism, was raised on the ruins of the formerly magnificent temple of the goddess Venus, and of deified Rome.

October

OF all the luminous and brilliant months of the year in Rome, October is the most exquisitely beautiful. It is St. Martin's Spring, closely followed by St. Martin's Summer. There is a scent of new wine in the air, and a hint of the coming chrysanthemums with their bitter fragrance.

October is so lovely that the Romans established the custom of going out into the hills every Thursday of that month for a picnic among the olives and the vines. So universal was the practice that a special name was invented for these October outings in the neighbourhood of the Eternal City: they were called *"Ottobrate"*. (Could one translate it as "Octoberations"? Or else more poetically as "Octoberings"?)

Inside the city the trees are beginning to turn to richest gold, as if to illustrate G. K. Chesterton's touching lines: "The pale leaf falls in pallor, But the green leaf turns to gold; We that had joy in being young, Shall have joy in growing old".

On the Janiculum, on the Pincian Hill and on the Aventine, people gather in groups, drawn by the irresistible attraction of the city lying beneath them in the glory of the autumn sun. And, while visiting these famous and frequented points, or "observatories" of the beauty of the city, the wise ones who know their Rome, ramble among the lesser-known parts of the city.

They go to little out-of-the-way inns where grapes hang heavy from vines growing so thickly on the beams of a pergola that they positively form a roof. Few visitors ever penetrate to these charming places, but "they're not so very, very far away". They are found, for example, in the *Trastevere,* along the Tiburtine Road, and near San Lorenzo.

The light that never was on sea or land seems to shine
in the mysterious *Trastevere,* the Land-Across-The-Tiber,
especially in October, and seems to radiate especially
from the church of *San Francesco a Ripa* (St.
Francis-on-the-River-Bank), where dear St. Francis himself lodged during one of his visits to Rome. There one

October sunshine on a bewildering sea of towers and domes

can see his cell and his portrait painted by a contemporary
artist; they carry one back into the legendary thirteenth
century, casting as it were, a golden-brown glow over the
city from his Feast-day on October 4th, on until the Feast
of All Saints.   And I think the glow is a radiance from
his brown habit.   It certainly appears to be one of the
causes of the glory of a Roman October.

Standing   on   the   Pincio,   whence   our   photograph

was taken, one looks down on a bewildering sea of roofs, domes and towers with the mighty cupola of St. Peter's etched (as a non-Catholic writer said) "like the crest of God against the flaming clouds of sunset".

The same writer continues: "St. Peter's, thus seen from afar, is the most superb embodiment in existence of Christianity towering in triumph upon the site of its agony and persecution. The city outspread beneath us seems like a stage where the history of half the world takes shape and re-enacts itself before our eyes. The Catholic Church is the oldest of all existing institutions. She has outlived and outfought the Empires of Augustus and Charlemagne. She has seen the transformation of the old world, and the discovery and upgrowth of the new. The boldest advances of thought, the most revolutionary discoveries of science, the most far-reaching developments of politics and economics, have failed to shake her power or modify her claims. One need not be oneself a Catholic to appreciate the intense interest of such a fact, and its profound possibilities for the history of the future."

Coming from a non-Catholic, this opinion is striking. Farther on he says: "Rome beckons to us, and who can stay indoors when the old Spanish steps are gay with flowers, and babies and their nurses fill the Villa Borghese with colour and laughter. Romance is waiting! Romance lurks in every doorway, peers from every palace-window, beckons mysteriously from every dark recess and narrow alley . . . Not unattended does one walk the streets of Rome: ghosts beyond number lurk by one's side . . . One thinks of St. Francis playing with the pet lamb of his friend Jacopa; of Petrarch crowned with laurel on the Capitol; of Fra Angelico painting ecstatically in the Vatican. The sun shines, the bells ring, and in the quiet air there hangs a mist of faintest red, as when one lets fall a drop of red wine into a cup of clear water . . . Venice for splendour, Florence for art, Naples for love and Rome for war, so runs the old saying. Not for nothing has she the She-wolf for her totem, with fangs bared and snarling defiance . . . Who shall say what red destiny may yet await her?"

The above was written in 1930.   Fourteen years later, the city was indeed saved from the "red ruin" of war, by the work and the prayers of one man, His Holiness Pope Pius XII.

Holy Week Ceremonies

WHERE shall we go in Holy Week if our time has not been fully organised in advance? This would be a unique opportunity for two or three friends to set out and explore Rome together, seeing for themselves something of the Romans at close quarters, realising the truth of what was once said by a foreigner after being present at a pilgrimage in which 15,000 Romans took part: "Well, certainly, Rome is very Catholic!"

On Palm Sunday we would suggest Mass at St. John Lateran; it is the Cathedral Church of Rome, where the functions are carried out to perfection. The ceremony of the Blessing of the Palms, with the procession and the singing of the *Gloria Laus* are a revelation of the meaning of the ceremony. The Lateran choir is second only to the Sistine choir.

On Wednesday one can make a beginning with *Tenebrae,* or at least a portion of that impressive office, if time does not allow attendance at the whole of it. On the three days that *Tenebrae* is sung one should go once to St. Peter's, once to the Jesuit church of the *Gesù* and once to the Benedictine *Sant' Anselmo.*

At St. Peter's the polyphonic rendering of the "Lamentations" is the supreme musical expression of grief. The long-drawn notes rise to the vast spaces of the arched vaulting and seem to hover there in the gloom, bewailing the sins of mankind. The singing at the *Gesù* is exceptionally good because for Holy Week the students of the German-Hungarian College are there to carry out all the ceremonies; and their musical training is perfect.

At *Sant' Anselmo* the International Benedictine College on the Aventine, one hears Gregorian chant at its best, and we advise lovers of it to be present for at least one of the

M

Holy Week functions, either in the morning or the afternoon.

The Cardinal Grand Penitentiary, proceeds formally to St. Mary Major on Wednesday afternoon, and to St. Peter's on Maundy Thursday and Good Friday. He sits on a

As the "Glorias" ring out on Easter Saturday the Romans
hasten to the fountains to bathe their eyes

special throne surrounded by his suite, and carries a golden rod, symbolic of his office. He touches the heads of the faithful who kneel before him with this rod, thereby allowing them to gain an indulgence of 300 days. This touch ("stroke" would be too strong a word) of the rod is a survival of the ancient custom of public penance imposed upon public sinners.

Some time during the week one should visit the Holy Stairs, which are close to St. John Lateran.

At the end of each of the functions of Holy Week the "Greater Relics" are shown at St. Peter's. A bell is rung and crowds are seen hastening to stand beneath the balcony which surmounts the statue of St. Veronica, near the Papal Altar. From that balcony a Canon of the basilica, in rochet and stole, blesses the faithful below, with the relics of the Passion which form one of the greatest treasures of the basilica; among them is the Veil of St. Veronica which bears the imprint of Our Lord's features, though at a distance it is very hard to see them.

On Maundy Thursday the ceremony of the Washing of the Feet is carried out by the Father Abbot of the Benedictines at St. Paul's-Outside-the-Walls; he washes and kisses the feet of twelve old men. As the Lateran Basilica is the Cathedral Church of Rome, the Cardinal Vicar celebrates Mass there and blesses the Holy Oils. Besides the usual ceremonies, Holy Orders are conferred on candidates for the priesthood; sometimes there are as many as a hundred to be ordained.

In the afternoon and evening of Maundy Thursday visitors from northern countries will probably be astounded at the devotion of the Romans visiting the Altars of Repose. Each of the four hundred churches is crowded with men, women and children, monks and nuns, rich and poor, praying fervently. The altars are beautifully arranged with flowers, plants, palms and candles. By six or seven in the evening there are queues outside the churches, even in the poorer parts of the city, while in front of the larger churches, there are not only queues but crowds awaiting their turn. The whole of Rome seems to turn out to do honour to Our Lord in the Blessed Sacrament.

On Good Friday one should go to the church of Holy Cross in Jerusalem, the Stational church, where the students of the French Seminary sing like angels.

On Holy Saturday, St. Peter's great bell leads the choir of all the bells of Rome which ring out at midday. If you should be on the Janiculum then, you will hear them in a mist of harmony, rising from the bell-towers below. And when the bells have finished you will see people hastening to the fountains to bathe their eyes. It is said that if you do this when you hear the bells on Easter Saturday, you will be free from eye trouble for the whole year, and your sight will be clear and keen. It is but one more sign of devotion to the glorious Resurrection of Jesus Christ, a sign of the joy of His children.

St. Philip and the Seven Churches

THE Feast of St. Philip Neri brings us to the charming custom which he inaugurated, that of the famous visit to the Seven Churches. Originally it was begun at mid-Lent as a counter-attraction of a spiritual nature to the worldly attractions of the Roman Carnival.

Now it takes place later, in the spring, when both the weather and growing things, flowers and foliage, are at their best. The pilgrimage is held regularly every year, and high-ranking prelates, priests and religious join the humbler folk in the long walk, interspersed with prayers, hymns, visits to the churches and picnic meals.

The expedition begins on a Saturday. In the evening the faithful meet at the tomb of St. Philip in the *Chiesa Nuova;* there follows a sermon explaining the significance of the visits, and booklets containing the exact itinerary, and hymns are distributed. Then, processionally, all go to St. Peter's to pray at the Tomb of the Apostle, stopping on the way to visit the sick in the ancient hospital of the Holy Spirit.

On Sunday morning the devotions begin bright and early. The meeting is at 7-30 at St. Paul's-Outside-the-Walls. For many this means leaving home at about 6-0. There Mass is said and all receive Holy Communion. After a light breakfast in the fields and gardens near the basilica, the procession forms and goes to the basilica and catacomb of St. Sebastian.

The road always taken from St. Paul's on the Ostian Way, to St. Sebastian's on the Appian Way, is still known as the Way of the Seven Churches (*Via delle Sette Chiese*) in remembrance of St. Philip.

From St. Sebastian's the pilgrims go to the church of SS. Nereus and Achilleus where they hear another Mass. Afterwards in the grassy spaces surrounding the towering walls of the Baths of Caracalla, they partake of a picnic dinner, and rest. During this period of relaxation there is music, poetry is recited, hymns are sung and the famous "Boy's Sermon" is preached by a little boy who has been appointed

The church of SS. Nereus and Achilleus near which St. Philip's pilgrims rested

beforehand. In other words a "Philippine Oratory" is held in the open air.

At 3-30 the march is resumed to St. John Lateran, followed by visits to the church of Holy Cross in Jerusalem, and St. Lawrence-outside-the-Walls, and ends at the basilica of St. Mary Major where Benediction of the Blessed Sacrament is given, and all separate, "tired but happy" as the ancient chronicle expresses it.

Pope Paul V ordained that the visits should be made solemnly in procession, and that the pilgrims should be divided into "centuries" or groups of one hundred; with a leader for each, who was to see that the hymns were sung in time and in tune, and that, at the resting-places all were properly provided with what they needed. We are told that sometimes the numbers of those who joined the expedition reached five thousand. At present the figure varies between one and two thousand.

St. Philip's success and the numbers he attracted in the visits to the Seven Churches, sad to say, got him into serious trouble with the *Vicariato,* or Roman Chancellor's office.

The Pope as Bishop of Rome appoints a Cardinal Vicar who overlooks those matters concerning discipline which are usually in the hands of the Bishop himself. Well, St. Philip was accused of wishing to form a new psalm-singing and peripatetic sect within the Church; it was said that under pretext of spirituality he was trying to gain personal popularity and high office, and the Cardinal Vicar called him severely to order, suspending him for the space of two weeks from saying Mass or hearing confessions.

The Saint submitted meekly, answering, as he pointed to the Crucifix: "He knows that I do not seek a personal following; for the glory of God I began the practice of visiting the Seven Churches, and now for the glory of God I give them up."

As soon as the accusation reached the ears of Pope Paul V, who was convinced of Philip's innocence as well as of his sanctity, he granted him full permission to continue this popular form of apostolate, adding that he gave his blessing willingly to the Saint and regretted deeply that he could not join in the pilgrimage himself. To his kind words he added the gift of two large gilded wax candles.

Wonderful accounts of the organisation of these visits are chronicled. It must have been no light matter to see that five thousand people were carefully provided with all that they needed. The old hymn-books show that the favourite hymn was St. Philip's own, with the refrain "Vanity of vanities, all is vanity".

In the seventeenth century the midday rest was taken in the famous Mattei Gardens attached to the Villa Celimontana on the Caelian Hill. The gardens were typical of the time, with their beautiful lawns, fountains, walks and flowers. Early in the morning the "Brothers" who took care of the material side of the proceedings— there were three hundred of them, all fervent disciples of the Oratory, and lusty fellows too—went to the Villa and began laying out the semi-circular enclosure for the Cardinals and dignitaries, and the places for the faithful at large The latter were seated three by three, around a sign which bore the number of the ticket each one had been given.

The Brethren brought to every group a special basket with three compartments in it. Each compartment contained: a loaf of bread; two big slices of Bologna sausage; a hard-boiled egg; half a cheese and two apples. In the centre of the basket was a large bottle of wine "carefully watered" says our chronicle, and a small packet of salt. Materials for quite a nice dinner; for by then the pilgrims were hungry.

Today, each one provides his own dinner, and it is probable that the President of the Workingmen's Retreats Associations, who issues the information and organises the pilgrimage, is not sorry that he is relieved from the duty of providing food for such a multitude.

Raphael's Resting Place in the Pantheon

THE Pantheon, later converted into the Church of St. Mary of the Martyrs, is the most noble former pagan temple in Rome, and the best-preserved. This, of course, is due to the fact that in the year 610, Pope St. Boniface consecrated it as a Christian church, transferred numbers of relics of the martyrs thither from the catacombs, and instituted the Feast of All Saints on the occasion.

Its preservation is also due to the fact that in the middle ages when the Senators took office they swore to defend the city against attack and especially to "defend the Tomb of the Apostle (i.e., St. Peter's), the fortress of Castel Sant' Angelo and the Pantheon".

It was built in the year 27 B.C. by Marcus Agrippa, friend and counsellor of Augustus, in honour of the seven most important gods in the mythological system of the time. The ample pillared portico has sixteen great columns of granite, each one thirty-six feet high, hewn from a single piece of stone.

The interior is circular, with a pavement of costly marbles. It is domed, and Michaelangelo said, when commissioned to re-build St. Peter's Basilica, that he would "raise the Pantheon on top of the Temple of Peace". He kept his word, for the diameter of the Pantheon is exactly that of the dome of St. Peter's. The "Temple of Peace" to which he alluded, was a famous and extensive temple in the Forum; but St. Peter's eventually was much larger and more important.

After it was consecrated as a Christian church, six of its fifteen altars were dedicated to Our Lady. The third side altar, to the left of the sanctuary, bears a marble statue of Our Lady executed in accordance with the last will of Raphael, one of the greatest painters the world has ever known (1483-1520).

Edward Hutton wrote of him: "Of all that imperious, splendid and lawless age, Raphael is the saviour. The presence of his nature is like a fair, soft, light over everything, or like a perfect flower in the midst of a battlefield. Rather than any soldier, or philosopher, or man of genius, he serves as the type of the Renaissance at its highest; and his failure—if so we may call it—is nothing more than the

A statue of Our Lady surmounts
Raphael's Tomb in the Pantheon

failure of all art to express, to do more than shadow forth that perfect state which Plato has seen lying in the heavens, and which St. Paul assures us, is there eternal."

The mortal remains of Raphael Sanzio lie beneath a low arched construction under a statue of Our Lady and her Child, in one of the niches formerly dedicated to a pagan god. On the right is a small oval recess containing a bust of the artist. Close to his tomb is that of Maria, niece of Cardinal Bibbiena, to whom he was engaged. Cardinal Bembo, a renowned Latinist, wrote his epitaph, which has been thus translated by Alexander Pope.

> *Living; great Nature feared he might outvie*
> *Her works; and dying, fears herself to die.*

It is not easy to understand why Pope used these lines in his epitaph of Sir Godfrey Kneller, with no acknowledgment as to the real author; but such things do happen.

Near Raphael are buried his friends and disciples: Baldassare Peruzzi, Taddeo Zuccari and Annibale Caracci.

Raphael was only 37 when he died, and the whole of Rome mourned his loss. His body lay in state for three days, and, when it was about to be lowered into the grave, Pope Leo X himself came to honour his memory. Kneeling down beside the body, weeping, he kissed the hand and prayed fervently for the repose of Raphael's soul.

The funeral ceremonies were among the most magnificent ever known, with Cardinals, dignitaries of all kinds and artists present at them. In the funeral procession, his greatest work, *The Transfiguration,* was carried before his bier.

A long poem on the funeral was written by Samuel Rogers (1763-1855) who is famous as the author of *Pleasures of Memory*. It expresses in stately language the sorrow of Rome on the death of the beloved painter. "When Raphael went—His heavenly face the mirror of his mind—His mind a temple for all lovely things—To flock and to inhabit; when he went—Wrapt in his sable cloak, the cloak he wore—To sleep beneath the venerable dome—('Twas on an April day, when Nature smiles)—All Rome was there. But ere the march began—Who had not sought him? And when all beheld—Him were he lay, how changed from yesterday—Him in that hour cut off, and at his head—His last great work. All were moved; and sighs burst forth, and loudest lamentations."

The Quirinal

THE QUIRINAL PALACE was planned and the construction begun in 1574, by Pope Gregory XIII (Ugo
Boncompagni), whose kindness towards St. Ignatius and
his early companions make him forever famous. Not
only did this great Pope encourage the Jesuits, but he
proved to be the benefactor of every enterprise directed
towards the education of the clergy. It was in 1579 that
he helped Dr. Allen (afterwards Cardinal) and Archdeacon
Owen Lewis, in the foundation of the "Venerable" English
College in Rome. Thus the English Martyrs are in a special
way connected with him by strong spiritual bonds.

Pope Gregory XIII chose this elevated position on the
summit of the Quirinal Hill for a new palace for two
reasons: in the first place he wished to build a residence
for the Popes where the summer heat would not be quite
as oppressive as at the low-lying Vatican Palace; and
secondly he intended, once and for all, to provide ample
quarters for the Cardinals and their suites who would
assemble in Rome for the election of a Pope. Arrangements
at the Vatican were complicated and unwieldy for such a
gathering, and the new palace would simplify everything,
with its permanent suites of rooms all opening off a long
corridor connected with a large chapel, and various halls
which could easily be cut off from the outer world.

The great portal, facing the obelisk, is surmounted by
fine statues of SS. Peter and Paul, and above them Our
Lady with the Holy Child. She and the Divine Infant were
placed there to bless the Pope who would stand on the
wide balcony beneath her, to give his blessing in turn,
"urbi et orbi". Elections of Popes were also announced
from that balcony. The last time it was thus used by a

Sovereign Pontiff was when Pope Pius IX gave his blessing to Italy in 1846.

In 1809 Pope Pius VII was removed by force from the Quirinal by Napoleon's orders. In 1870, when the Kingdom of Italy was proclaimed, it became the Royal Palace for the Kings of the House of Savoy. Now it is the residence

The Quirinal Palace—built for the Popes, occupied by Kings and now taken over by the President

for the President of the Italian Republic. One wonders how many more changes history has in store for the great building and if it will eventually return to the Holy See.

The Quirinal is the third of the great Pontifical residences in Rome. First, the Popes dwelt in the Lateran Palace, next to the Lateran Basilica; after their return from Avignon in 1377, they took up their abode in the Vatican Palace; and in 1580, Pope Sixtus V established his court definitely at the Quirinal, where he died in 1590.

It was Sixtus V who placed the great obelisk in the centre of the open space in front, and flanked it with two famous statues of Castor and Pollux, the twin gods of the old legend. These statues are remarkable examples of Greek sculpture and are held by some to be the work of Pheidias and Praxiteles. In front of them a powerful jet of water rises in a granite basin and splashes over the sides with a sound grateful to the ears in the hot summer days.

From the square there is a magnificent view of Rome, with St. Peter's on the sky-line; and it is always a favourite resort for mothers and nurses with babies in search of sun and air.

The building itself is much more extensive than it appears, as it stretches for about four hundred feet along the street on the right of the spectator. This is known as the "long sleeve" by the Romans; the apartments in it are neither elaborate nor artistic. However, the Chapel of the Popes in the block facing the fountain, is of singular beauty, as are the gardens which are extensive and well-kept.

The Charm of Rome's Cloisters

THERE are numbers of cloisters in Rome, each with its own special character and charm. Pilgrims should bear in mind that whenever they visit a church they would do well to enquire if there is a cloister attached to it. In seeing cloisters that they discover for themselves, they will enrich their memories with a unique experience of beauty, while enjoying a sense of personal achievement.

The origin of cloisters is simple. When St. Benedict established monastic life in the west, the monks found that they needed a sheltered space to walk in when the weather was bad, and also a large connecting passage leading to their various meeting-places such as the church, the refectory and the chapter house. So the cloisters, as it were, followed the monks; and establishments served by monks or friars, by degrees became possessed of cloisters.

A pilgrim, particularly sensitive to beauty in all its forms, wrote as follows about the cloister of the Lateran Basilica: "Silence was the only possible greeting that we could give to the sight that met us as we entered. Shafts of evening light slanted through slender coupled columns and turned the grey pavement to gold. Green palm leaves waved behind them. The delicate columns were ornamented with every imaginable form of twisted ribbon-mosaic designs. Here and there they were geometrical, sometimes they were plain and devoid of ornament as if to provide a contrast to the more elaborate ones. Above them a mosaic architrave showed exquisite tracery.

"The evening light revealed an unearthly charm in everything, investing the whole enclosure with a fantastically ethereal quality that of itself imposed silence. We stood there, hardly daring to move, as if the vision, like spun glass, would be shattered by the slightest motion, while mauve shadows gathered on the stone paving."

The genius of the "Roman Marble-Workers" as they

were called, led them to execute such works. They were builders, mosaic workers, stone carvers and masons, all in one. Two great families of such artists dominated Rome from the eleventh to the fourteenth century; the Cosmati

The Cloisters of St. Paul's-Outside-the-Walls

and the Vassallecti. This we know, for numbers of their works such as cloisters, canopies over the central altars in basilicas, pulpits and pavements, or arches over entrances bear inscriptions such as "John and Luke, sons of Cosmas, Roman stone cutters did this work".

There is a famous example of their decoration in the tombs of Edward the Confessor and of King Henry III in Westminster Abbey, for their men penetrated even to the Northern Isles. Their inspiration shows the influence of classical models, though it is overlaid and transformed by the fever and fantasy of the Gothic, and Oriental colour and brilliance from Byzantium.

In the cloister of the Lateran many significant relics of the past are preserved.   Perhaps the most interesting of all is what looks like a table of porphyry supported on four columns, about six feet high. It is said to have been brought back from the Holy Land by the Crusaders, and that it indicates the exact height of Our Blessed Lord.   It certainly appears to be the height of a man, but taller than the figure of Our Saviour is generally represented.

The cloister at St. Paul's-Outside-the-Walls, shows the play of light and shade to perfection, as well as the variety of the columns and the decoration of the inner side of the arches.   In the spandrels of the arches facing the cloister garth (that is in the small spaces between the shoulders of the arches and the inscription which runs above them) are many delightful and fantastic ornaments, such as flowers, faces or figures.   The most famous of all these is a scene, in which a wolf, disguised as a monk, with an imposing volume in front of him, is solemnly preaching to a goat.

Romance walks forever in the small rose-coloured cloister of St. Lawrence-Outside-the-Walls.   It is simpler and much less ornate than those of St. John Lateran and of St. Paul's. But, what character!   It was built for the Cistercians in the twelfth century, and reflects their spirit of austerity joined to a sweet and gentle piety.   The brick walls are really of a deep rose-colour, particularly at sunset.   The balustrade is much lower than those of the two preceding examples, and this gives an air of intimacy and informality to the place; the columns are single instead of coupled, and are severely plain.   Palms, magnolias, roses, flowering shrubs, irises and geraniums run riot in the garden of the central court, where a fountain splashes softly.   The sons of St. Francis are now in charge, and everything here reflects their Founder's love of nature.

Many fragments of ancient catacomb inscriptions are kept in this cloister together with remnants of medieval carvings. Today there is one "souvenir" there which came to *San Lorenzo* in 1943: a huge fragment of one of the bombs which wrecked the basilica itself. Happily, amid the destruction of the neighbouring slum quarter, the cloister was untouched, and there the Friars sheltered the homeless until dwellings could be found for them.

Even in those tragic days when whole families huddled together under the old roof for protection, it seemed as if the Franciscan spirit of peace still hovered among the arches, in spite of fear, pain and misery. The Capuchin Fathers were truly all things to all men, and opened their hearts as well as their cloister to suffering humanity.

The English College

EVEN to those who have never been to Rome the words "The English College" bring a thrill of recognition and affection; and perhaps still more thrilling is the name "The *Venerabile*", by which title it is known on account of its antiquity, for it is one of the oldest in the Eternal City.

The College is the lineal descendant of a hospice established in the early middle ages for the reception of Saxon pilgrims. The line of pilgrims from Great Britain stretches back uninterruptedly to about sixty years after the landing of St. Augustine and his monks; and when King Ine came to Rome in 726 the "English Colony" was already a distinct body occupying a special district.

With the passing of the centuries the "hospice" developed and took various forms, and among its inmates were pilgrims, statesmen, prelates and some students.

However, the College as such—that is to say, a seminary for "Mass priests"—was founded by William Allen, aided by his friend Archdeacon Owen Lewis and a group of Catholic gentlemen; it was opened formally at Christmas in the year 1578, thanks to the support and encouragement of Pope Gregory XIII.

St. Philip Neri was active in Rome at the time, and we are told that, on meeting the students in the streets, he would take off his hat respectfully and greet them with the words: "Hail, flowers of martyrdom". He was also accustomed to bestow a special blessing on them when they were departing for their dangerous mission in England. These scenes are beautifully represented in Shrewsbury Cathedral.

The College underwent many vicissitudes in penal times, and much hardship was endured by its inmates. There was a respite in 1676 when Cardinal Howard, a Dominican who was its "Protector", munificently reconstructed the ancient buildings enlarging them at the same time.   In the eighteenth century the College again went through a stormy and difficult period; according to the chronicles,

The entrance to the English College
and the exterior of the Chapel

between 1775 and 1798 only seven students were ordained. Notwithstanding, it managed to survive, only to encounter the tragedy of seizure by the French troops during the Napoleonic occupation of Rome.

Finally, in 1817, when the Napoleonic domination was ended and order restored, Robert Gradwell, at the wish of the English Bishops, was appointed Rector. He came to a heritage of bare walls in the College, no students and utter confusion in what concerned finances.

But we are told that in a very few years he had not only repaired the buildings, cleared the financial jungle and made the College solvent, but also brought up a hardy generation of students and gained for them an amazing reputation in Roman circles. Gradwell was indeed the second founder of the *"Venerabile"*, a man of outstanding greatness and heroic mould.

He was succeeded by Nicholas Wiseman to whom the students always looked up with affectionate reverence as to a ruler whose warm heart matched his glowing genius. He was particularly anxious that those under him should reap the fullest advantage from their stay in the Eternal City, and used to take them to churches, catacombs, galleries, museums and places of cultural and historical interest. He gave the students a devoted love of Rome and of the Holy See, and his memory is held in benediction.

Space will not allow mention of the various Rectors who followed Wiseman, until we reach the year 1917. On that date an ecclesiastic who left a great name, became Rector of the College: Monsignor Arthur Hinsley.

One of his first problems was to find a country house to take the place of that at Monte Porzio which the College had possessed for two centuries. The gaining of the property at Palazzola in 1920 was one of the happiest episodes in the life of the College, a triumph of prayer and careful negotiation.

Among other reforms at this time, few have been so quickly and lastingly successful as that of his installing a community of nuns, with their own separate quarter of the building, to look after the kitchen and the laundry of the entire establishment. To him the College also owes the cherished privilege of a skilfully contrived swimming-pool at one end of the garden in Rome, as well as the comfort of central heating when the chilly *tramontana* wind blows down from the surrounding mountains.

In 1935 Mgr. Hinsley succeeded Cardinal Bourne as Archbishop of Westminster, and it was in the College he loved that he received the *biglietto* appointing him to the dignity of Cardinal, in December 1937.

Dr. William Godfrey (now Archbishop of Liverpool) succeeded him and made a number of valuable improvements both in Rome and at Palazzola.

In 1939, when war broke out in Europe, it was decided that the students, headed by the Vice-Rector, Mgr. Richard Smith (the Rector being already in England on business) should depart. With wonderful swiftness and efficiency all preparations were made: treasures from the sacristy and the library were taken to the Vatican for safe keeping, and the premises were leased to the Knights of Malta to be used as a military hospital. The College and staff were then housed in St. Mary's Hall, Stonyhurst, thanks to the kindness of the Jesuit Fathers.

Finally, in October, 1946, the College came back to its old quarters in the beloved and noisy *Via Monserrato*. Once there, the number of students rose to the former level and the old ways were quickly resumed.

Today the College, surrounded by the affection of English pilgrims, maintains its famous traditions of hospitality and is always the rallying-point of England's Catholicism in the Church's capital. It is ever true to the character of its foundation and to the teaching of its glorious array of confessors and martyrs.

The Trevi Fountain

YES, you have guessed it. If you want to come back to Rome you must, before you leave, throw some coins into the Trevi Fountain. A hundred years ago people said that you should drink its water in order to be sure to come back.

Perhaps someone who has been in Rome recently, will object that since the war there have been no coins, but only paper money, and one doesn't visualise paper money doing any good if it were to be thrown into the miniature lake in front of those waterfalls. Well, by the time you get here, coins will probably be again in circulation, and the reputation of the ancient fountain will be safe.

The fountain deserves much more than a passing glance. It is a real masterpiece of late Renaissance art, erected in 1735 by Nicolò Bracci, under the Pontificate of Clement XII. Bracci started with the façade of the Palace of the Dukes of Poli which has three pilasters and two great Corinthian columns on either side; between them are two rows of windows with balconies.

It was a formal *palazzo,* in the grand manner, with nothing at all "sylvan" about it. But it was the fashion in those days to build imitation ruins in ducal parks, and so nothing would do but that Neptune with his tritons and sea-horses should appear in the heart of the city in front of a very stately palace.

The noise of the rushing waters was to be as the roar of the sea. And so it is to this day. In the centre of the façade, the architect designed a great niche wherein he placed a statue of Neptune, god of the sea, in a fine shell-chariot drawn by prancing, or rather splashing, sea-horses, driven madly along by two of Neptune's tritons or subordinate deities; one of them is blowing a conch-shell, the other is apparently having trouble with his unmanageable sea-horse.

The classic statues which flank Neptune in the centre, represent Abundance and Health. Above them are two panels with interesting bas-reliefs, one of which shows the legendary maiden directing Agrippa's thirsty soldiers to the spring near Trevi whence the water flowed; the other

A general view of the Trevi Fountain, with the Poli Palace in the background

representing the Emperor approving the design of the aqueduct which was to bring this spring water into the city; the same spring water, of course, still flows in the fountain. The four topmost statues symbolise the four seasons.

The plan of the water, if such it can be called, is remarkable. There is one main central series of basins whence it flows, or rather overflows quietly, finally reaching what looks like a miniature lake. (That is where you throw your money.) But the side issues are much more interesting, for on either flank of the sea-horses, rocks have been placed in the most fantastic disorder possible. It looks as if an earthquake had disrupted a small cliff causing water to burst out of the fissures. Snowy foaming jets gush from crevices, leaping, dashing and tumbling; some little rivulets run wild splashing their glistening drops over rocks, marine monsters and stone vegetation. In a corner, one tiny stream flows quietly and sedately, and the builders thoughtfully placed a smooth stone beneath it for the convenience of thirsty tourists and passers-by. It is "drinkable" according to a small sign placed near it.

The little square in front of the fountain, is one of the most animated places in Rome, filled with stalls of vegetable and fruit-sellers, and push-carts with every kind of merchandise imaginable; also loungers, not to mention pilgrims and tourists. The latter turn their backs resolutely to the fountain and throw their money in, it is necessary to throw the coins over your shoulder for the charm to work.

Facing the fountain is a graceful little Renaissance church dedicated to the Martyrs SS. Vincent and Anastasius, built by the famous Cardinal Mazarin. Being close to the Quirinal, this was the parish church of the Popes when they resided there. In those days it was the custom to remove the heart from the body of a deceased Pope before embalming it, therefore the hearts of all the Popes who reigned from 1590 to 1903 are preserved in urns in the crypt of SS. Vincent and Anastasius, that is to say from Pope Sixtus V to Pope Leo XIII.

It is an easy walk from the Trevi Fountain to the famous *Via del Corso* where the church dedicated to Pope St. Marcellus enshrines the great miraculous Crucifix of Rome. On special occasions this crucifix is transferred to St. Peter's for veneration. The procession is extraordinarily impressive, it usually takes place by torchlight, the Crucifix being borne on a movable altar drawn by six black horses.

o

There are several other renowned crucifixes in the city; especially venerated is one enshrined in a small chapel directly above the Mamertine prison, which closely associates Our Lord's death on the Cross with the sufferings of the martyrs imprisoned beneath.

In Honour of the Blessed Trinity

THE church of the *Trinità dei Monti* stands at the top of the famous Spanish Steps, and is known throughout the world, not only because of its intrinsic importance, but because it is closely connected with the Convent of the Sacred Heart where generations of schoolgirls of all nationalities have been educated. The Convent was the Roman residence of St. Madeleine Sophie Barat, Foundress of the Society of the Sacred Heart. Cornelia Connelly, Foundress of the Society of the Holy Child Jesus, also lived there for some time. Its history is as interesting as it is little known, and goes back to a hermit in Calabria (the toe of the "boot" of Italy), born in the city of Paola, in 1416.

Francis, for such was his name, lived as a hermit from the age of 14 to 19 years; then, as he was joined by several companions, built a little monastery and a church. Many are the miraculous occurrences related in connection with Francis of Paola, among others that of having crossed the Straits of Messina borne on his cloak.

Pope Sixtus IV, in Rome, wished to ordain him a priest, but he refused. However, he could not refuse the Pope's order to go to France at the request of the dying King Louis XI, a shrewd, cruel and superstitious ruler, yet possessed of faith and craving the presence of a saint at his deathbed.

When Louis XI died at Tours, Francis remained there and founded another house of his Order, in which he died in 1507, having been protected and encouraged by three successive Kings of France. He was later canonised at the request of a fourth.

We learn that in the year 1403 two French Minims came to Rome. The Order was called by this name because the Founder was not content with his brethren being "minor" or "lesser"; they must be "minims", that is, "the least".

These two religious bore letters from Charles VIII, King of France; therefore the French Ambassador to the Holy See bought a fine piece of land for them on the Pincian

The Church of the Trinita dei Monti and the Spanish Steps

Hill, known as "the hill of gardens", for even then it was one of the most beautiful localities in the city.

The Minims began to build their church when King Charles VIII was present in Rome. From that time the plot was considered as French property. In the following centuries the church and monastery were finished, and a beautiful cloistered court elaborately frescoed and decorated completed the monastery.

In 1726 the superb flight of "Spanish Steps", with lordly

curves and terraces was built to give better access to the church. In 1828, Pope Leo XII proposed to the French Ambassador that the property of the *Trinità dei Monti* with all its buildings, should be given to the Ladies of the Sacred Heart as a school for girls, since the Minims found it no longer suitable for their purpose.

Via Condotti is a narrow street, like a telescope trained on *Piazza di Spagna*. The square and steps are called "Spanish" because in the square was, and still is, situated the palace of the Spanish Ambassador to the Holy See. Coming just before dusk along *Via Condotti* towards the *Trinità,* one can grasp the full beauty of the whole scene, a beauty of atmosphere and of colour, in the splendour which the sunset lays upon the square itself, as well as on the steps and the twin-towered church. In that magic hour it looks like an acropolis of silver and moonstone, stained with delicate mauve, rose and pearl grey.

At night, no less a writer and traveller than Edward Hutton, is content to find that marvellous staircase the most beautiful thing in Rome. In the daytime he finds it too noisy with people, too colourful with its banks of flowers (but so many others love the steps all the more on account of those barricades of flowers), too bright, too real. On the other hand, he says: "In twilight and darkness, when it is deserted by all, its grave lines, so cunningly sumptuous, seem almost ascetic and very quiet in their ample beauty, leading one slowly, with dignity, with many well-timed pauses, to the summit. And then, too, the mere stucco of the beautiful church to which it serves as a threshold or atrium is lost in the generous beauty of night. One might think it indeed to be of marble, or some precious unheard-of stone, chrysoprase or amber, jasper or chalcedony, or ivory and pallid gold. It suggests the ecstasy of a great French building restrained by the sanity of the sun."

Something of the fantastic beauty of the spot is found also on the Pincio, the continuation of the "hill of gardens".

It is the favourite walk of Romans, especially at sunset, when St. Peter's may be seen at its most glorious in an aureole of "purple and ashes of roses, cinnamon, umber and dun".

The northern part of this same hill was once occupied by the famous *Horti Aciliani,* that is to say the palace and gardens of the Acilii Glabriones, a noble family of ancient lineage. One of them led the victorious Roman Army in 191 B.C.; and later, at the time of the martyrdom of St. Peter, one of them was Praetor. However, in the succeeding years, a number of them were converted to Christianity, and their tombs were discovered about forty years ago in the Catacomb of Priscilla.

Manlius Acilius Glabrio, who had been a Consul under Trajan, was publicly accused of being "a promoter of novelty in religion" and was condemned by Domitian to wrestle with two bears in the amphitheatre. Victorious over both animals, he was exiled, and finally gained the crown of martyrdom. The "novelty" was Christianity.

So we leave the *Trinità* and the *Pincio* with the glow of sunset still lingering in the evening sky, while the bells of the city sound the *Ave Maria,* and the silvery voices of the Roman fountains join in the prayer.

Index

Printed in Great Britain by
Samuel Walker (Printers & Publishers), Ltd., Hinckley, Leics.